At the lowest point in my life, when I didn't even want to live because my marriage and family were a mess, all I could do was to cry out to God and ask Him for help to find some peace and hope. I soon learned that God was there to help me through the Holy Spirit and Jesus inside me. I began to understand that they would be the anchor that would never leave me, even though the rest of world would still be a mess. These same principles have been taught at Mercy for over thirty years to broken young women. My good friend Nancy Alcorn is the founder and president of Mercy. In Nancy's new book, *Ditch the Baggage, Change Your Life*, she gives practical and easy-to-understand lessons for anyone seeking the peace and hope that I once sought—principles that are keys to lasting freedom. Take a step onto the path toward peace and hope that are yours to have and get this book today!

—KAY ROBERTSON
COSTAR, *DUCK DYNASTY*

Real. Practical. Life-changing! In this book Nancy Alcorn unpacks the truth about the "baggage" we all have and how God wants us to be free from carrying all that old stuff around. But how do you get free? This book is the best, clearest, and most complete explanation of where lasting freedom comes from and exactly how that can be sorted out in your own life. I have known Nancy for many years and have seen these principles taught in the Mercy homes worldwide. Now her new book, *Ditch the Baggage, Change Your Life*, is available so that all of us can utilize these principles in our own lives as well as help others find lasting freedom. This book is a must-have for all pastors and really anyone who works with people in any capacity!

—JOHN BURNS
AUTHOR, SPEAKER, AND PASTOR AT RELATE CHURCH

As the founder and publisher of a nationally circulated magazine, I often have deeply committed Christians writing to me who are miserable in their current situation. Many of these people even know that God has a better plan for them but do not have a clue on how to get out of their misery, despair, and heartache. If this describes you, I have great news for you! Nancy Alcorn's book *Ditch the Baggage, Change Your Life* takes you through a process of healing straight from His Word. She makes things so simple and very clear—all with the experience of seeing this work in the lives of thousands of young women who have come through her program at Mercy. Your heart will be healed and you will gain victory in your life as you read Nancy's new book and work through these principles. I am sure of it!

—LAINE LAWSON CRAFT
FOUNDER AND PUBLISHER, *WHOAWOMEN* MAGAZINE

DITCH
the BAGGAGE
CHANGE YOUR LIFE

DITCH
the BAGGAGE
CHANGE YOUR LIFE

NANCY ALCORN

CHARISMA
HOUSE

Cover design by Studio Gearbox
Design Director: Justin Evans

Visit the author's website at www.mercymultiplied.com.

Some names, places, and identifying details with regard to stories in this book have been changed to help protect the privacy of individuals who may have been involved or had similar experiences.

Library of Congress Cataloging-in-Publication Data:
Alcorn, Nancy.
  Ditch the baggage, change your life / by Nancy Alcorn. -- First edition.
     pages cm
  ISBN 978-1-62998-012-6 (trade paper) -- ISBN 978-1-62998-013-3 (e-book)
  1. Change (Psychology)--Religious aspects--Christianity. I. Title.
  BV4599.5.C44A43 2015
  248.4--dc23
                                    2014048626

15 16 17 18 19 — 9 8 7 6 5 4 3 2
Printed in the United States of America

DEDICATION

This book is dedicated to all who are hurting, desperate, and looking for an answer. There is hope for you. There is an answer! This book is also dedicated to people who are reaching out to others who are struggling. Thank you for being willing to stand in the gap and help those who are hurting. My prayer is that you will find direction, guidance, and answers through the pages of this book.

CONTENTS

ACKNOWLEDGMENTS

JOEL KILPATRICK—WITHOUT YOUR expertise and belief in our mission, this book would not have been possible. Thank you for pushing me to dig deep and share these principles of freedom with the masses.

Melanie Carter—for your tireless editing, attention to detail, and solid belief in this project.

Christy Singleton—for providing an invaluable sounding board for key points in this book.

Mercy staff—for willingly sharing your own personal stories of healing for use in this book.

All the counselors at Mercy and the young women who have come through the program—for being the model and example of how these principles work, and for encouraging and inspiring me through your stories of freedom and restoration.

FOREWORD

I HAVE BEEN PERFORMING GOSPEL MUSIC for many years and have had the chance to be in front of all kinds of audiences. I have always felt that I am best using my gifts for God when my voice is being used to minister to hurting people. Over the years, I have had the great fortune to meet others who are committed to helping the lost and broken, and one of my very favorite people who shares this passion with me is Nancy Alcorn.

I have known Nancy for over fifteen years and have followed her ministry. Year after year incredibly hurt and broken young women come into Mercy and leave completely transformed! I have had Nancy speak at my conference on several occasions because I have seen the results of the keys to freedom that she gleans from God's Word, which are able to help people—both inside and outside the walls of Mercy. I am so incredibly pleased that she has finally taken the time to share the very principles of healing that Mercy uses with the rest of the world through her new book, *Ditch the Baggage, Change Your Life.*

Nancy Alcorn and Mercy are not afraid to deal with the ugly, tough stuff—sexual abuse, self-harm, eating disorders, drug addictions. Nancy says that if you can get to the core issues behind someone's behavior, you can help a person heal from the inside out! But the real healing comes when people realize the truth about God and His love for us and how we can use the tools and keys from the Bible to be fully restored!

If you work with people who are hurting or if you are struggling yourself, God wants us to be free! In this book Nancy guides you through a process that will help you move toward that very freedom.

—CeCe Winans
GRAMMY–winning recording artist

INTRODUCTION

I WAS VISITING ONE of the more prominent churches in a certain city and enjoying the privilege of speaking to the congregation about the work we do at Mercy—helping young women find freedom from all kinds of painful, crazy, and mixed-up life experiences. After the service an older woman approached me and leaned in close with tears streaming down her cheeks. She looked very well put together, but the tears left little trails in her makeup. "I had an abortion years ago and have never forgiven myself," she said softly so nobody else could hear. "Will you pray for me?" I could feel the pain emanating from her heart, though it was well hidden under the nice clothes and the look of success we Americans like to project. I prayed with her that she would choose to forgive herself as God already had forgiven her, and that her heart would finally heal from the pain she had carried for so long.

After we prayed, a young woman came up. Her eyes were like deep pools of regret. "I wish I had known about your ministry last year," she said. "I've been living with the choices I made and ... it's so hard." We prayed together that she would freely receive the Father's mercy for what was in her past as well.

Next a father came up. He looked successful, the kind of guy you might see driving around town in a nice car who seems to have it all together.

"It's my daughter," he said, sighing deeply. "She's on drugs and can't seem to shake it. It's wrecking her life. We worry about her night and day. She's had several abortions already and—I'm wondering, please, would you call her? She's scheduled to have her third or fourth abortion tomorrow. We're just desperate. Maybe if she hears what God has done in other people's lives, she will keep this baby."

Those stories I heard in that flagship church in a major American city were exactly like the stories I hear everywhere I go. Be it a church, a mall, any workplace or restaurant in the United States, people carry untold stories of unresolved pain. "I wish I had heard this message and known about Mercy when I was going through what I went through," they say to me. "I would have made a completely different choice and lived in freedom rather than bondage for all these years." Some pull me aside and tell me about things from their past that nobody else knows—violence or sexual abuse in their childhood and other painful things. "Now it's causing problems in my marriage," they say. "Please help."

At Mercy we get calls from women and men in their forties and fifties dealing with the same things teenagers are going through. No matter how put together or un-put together somebody looks, our problems and fears are the same. We all stumble in many ways, the Bible says, and the enemy's snares don't distinguish between our bank accounts, clothing, parenting abilities, and church backgrounds.

I've learned not to be surprised by the outward appearance of anyone who shares a deeply held secret with me. In fact, the people who look the most put-together often have the hardest time breaking free because there's more at stake when admitting their problem. They are like marathon runners determined to keep running because they aren't "supposed" to have problems—and they're wearing themselves out on the inside. It's easier, they think, to let the momentum of life keep them busy than to unshackle themselves from past pain.

The problem is that while most of the time it may seem dormant, that pressure is still there like a volcano waiting to blow. Sometimes it erupts into real-life problems, attitudes, and reactions, creating fresh heartaches. Those struggling may not even know their pain is related to the original offense. They just know they do things they don't want to do.

That brings me to you. You may have journeyed through some traumatic seasons of life as well. If so, welcome to the human race. Some of those experiences may have driven you into life-controlling addictions or bad behaviors. Others may have simply caused you to struggle repeatedly with emotions and habits that limit and control your life, even at what may seem like a low level. Perhaps you see yourself in the following descriptions of these people I have encountered:

- ❈ The helicopter mom who constantly fusses over her children—and grandchildren, husband, the neighbor's kids—out of a driving need to provide safety and guidance.

- ❈ The career-focused young man whose ambitions leave him without patience, and whose entire self-image is wrapped up in what he's able to accomplish.

- ❈ The woman who finds herself exercising obsessively and doesn't seem to understand why.

- ❈ Men and women whose default emotion is sadness and loss, feelings that are present even when life is going well.

- ❈ The career woman who must control every detail of her life or she flies off the handle.

❀ The "acceptable addict" who must have caffeinated drinks or pain-relief pills or prescription medications to make it through a day.

❀ The man or woman who doesn't build lasting friendships because he or she can't open up to other people because of fear.

❀ The person who thinks all the time about food and eats either too much or too little.

❀ The dad who comes home and plays video games for hours alone, ignoring his family.

❀ The person who goes ballistic when a spouse or girlfriend or boyfriend doesn't regularly text where they are.

I have known many of these people—and have fit some of these descriptions myself. Life is full of struggles, and our struggles are often invisible to others. We become skilled at performing our part at work and home as if nothing is wrong despite what's going on inside. Our pain may come from wounds as fresh as yesterday or as deep as a lifetime ago.

Let me get you thinking. What do you identify with in the list below?

❀ A high need to control situations and people

❀ Anger over little things

❀ Anxiety about money and relationships

❀ Weight consciousness

❀ Fitness obsession

❀ Concerns about reputation

- Money—fear of losing it and a driving desire for more
- Substance reliance
- Self-hatred
- Lying
- Manipulation
- Self-promotion
- Lack of care and concern for others
- A sharp tongue
- Violent reactions
- A time-consuming hobby
- A critical attitude
- High walls and the inability to make lasting friends
- A distrust of authority
- Phobias
- The need to provide everything your child or family wants

Certainly each of us could circle a few things on that list. But I believe the Holy Spirit is pinpointing one or two struggles in your own life right now that He would like to release you from. For some people, freedom means walking away from a terrible memory or experience such as a divorce, rape, car accident, or other major trauma. For others, freedom means getting unstuck from life-sapping thoughts or behaviors that keep you from flourishing in your walk with Christ and your relationships with others. God's principles of freedom apply to everyday struggles as well as "big" things. So many people are stuck in fear, annoyance, unforgiveness, or control.

Is that struggle you're having causing relational problems? Health problems? Is it keeping you from accomplishing what God has called you to in this season of life? Do you feel like you walk in peace and love and gentleness? Or the opposite?

I like what my friend Debbie Harvie says about identifying trouble areas in our lives: it's only a problem when it's a problem. The Bible says it is for freedom that Christ has set us free (Gal. 5:1). Freedom is not found in secret habits or obsessive thought patterns. Freedom is found by living in the fruit of the Spirit (Gal. 5:22–23):

- Love
- Joy
- Peace
- Patience
- Kindness
- Goodness
- Faithfulness
- Gentleness
- Self-control

Now turn those upside down. Are you experiencing the opposite of the fruit of the Spirit? Things like:

- Diminished feelings of love and trouble forming deep relationships
- Constant unsettledness

❀ Impatience

❀ Sharp words and irritation

❀ Vulgarity and bad intentions toward others

❀ Lying, deception, or not keeping your word

❀ Rough or violent reactions

❀ Self-indulgence or inability to control certain behaviors

This book has one simple message that many people have been waiting a lifetime to hear: you were born to live free—and by God's grace I will help you do it. The approach I use is not novel or new; it's biblical, it's doable, and it is the most practical and effective way to walk in freedom. I have taken many people down this path. No matter what you have experienced in the past, or what you are experiencing right now, it is your right as a follower of Christ to walk in freedom all of the time. As you learn to follow this path of freedom it will redefine your life. You will release thoughts and feelings and habits that have dogged you. You will live life as it is supposed to be lived in Christ.

I can speak boldly into your situation because for more than thirty years I have worked with women ages thirteen to twenty-eight who struggle with some of the worst things someone can experience in life: self-harming habits, starvation, suicide, addictions, unplanned pregnancies, sexual abuse, violence, and more. These kinds of behaviors and their causes are more common than you might expect, though for many of us they can seem extreme. But by helping women find freedom in these "extreme" situations we have found the pathway to freedom for everyone. Ours is a rubber-meets-the-road ministry. I don't have a lot of patience for talking about a problem without solving it. The apostle Paul said the kingdom of God is not in talk but in power (1 Cor. 4:20). I believe that one hundred percent.

In this book I take those same tools that allow girls to walk out of personal prisons and give them to you—normal people, moms and dads, working people, people in ministry, students, men and women, old and young, whoever you are. Every person reading these words can simply and effectively experience lasting freedom in Christ. I know it will work for you. It is your inheritance.

One girl at our home went from being a stripper to being a pastor's wife, and thousands of others have broken free of life-controlling and sometimes-deadly behaviors. Girls walk through the doors of our homes looking like they've been run over by a city bus and leave as the most "normal" looking people you can imagine, with vibrant and confident hearts in Christ. I never cease to wonder at the transformation.

That's the transformation I will be leading you through in these pages.

In secular treatment, the focus is on changing behavior, which is temporary and gives surface results. I'm here to tell you that behavior modification is not the answer. It offers no heart change. I spent eight years working in corrections in Tennessee and not once did I see behavior modification lead to lasting life change. That's why I left to start Mercy in 1983. Since then we have helped thousands of girls find freedom with these simple but transforming truths. You see, Jesus did not come to modify our behavior; He came to transform our lives. He promised that "He who believes in Me, as the Scripture has said, out of his heart shall flow rivers of living water'" (John 7:38). He meant that your heart can flow with the freedom and peace He makes available to you right now.

Consider this your handbook for freedom, your guide to personal liberation in Christ. The title, *Ditch the Baggage, Change*

Your Life, is a useful analogy for those of us trying to navigate through life. If you have flown on an airplane lately you know that taking baggage along has gotten expensive. It used to be that bags flew free. You could check two bags for free and carry on a couple of items, if the gate attendant overlooked them. Now the airlines charge you for each bag you check and some even charge for carry-ons! The more baggage you bring, the more expensive your trip.

The parallel is obvious: baggage is expensive when we fly, and personal baggage is expensive in our lives as well. We weren't designed to have the baggage of regrets, unresolved pain, and bad habits that we drag from place to place, from relationship to relationship like a sack of old junk. How many times have you arrived at your physical destination, opened your suitcase and thought, "Why did I even bring that? Who needs a parka in Florida in July?" It's the same in our personal lives. Imagine the freedom you would feel traveling without any baggage at all because when you arrived at your destination everything was provided for you. That's the feeling of freedom we should have in Christ. I'm eager to show you the path.

Let me say in advance that I love and admire you for seeking advice and help in this book, and I encourage you to go all the way with it. Invest yourself in it and see what the Lord does with you. I bet you'll be surprised. In fact, I look forward to hearing from you about how this book impacted your journey and transformed your heart, by God's grace.

So let's set our hearts to overcome the past and soar to places we've only dreamed of before. For some of you it will be a radical departure from the life you live now. For others it will seem more like a course correction. In every case it will liberate you to be and do what you haven't been and done before. This path of freedom will profoundly impact your thoughts and emotions, your relationships with others, and your closeness to God.

I've said it many times: if we do not deal with our issues, our issues will deal with us. So get ready. It's time to ditch the baggage.

Chapter 1

KEY #1: TOTAL COMMITMENT TO FREEDOM

ONE NIGHT WHEN I was working for the State of Tennessee as an investigator of emergency child abuse cases, we got a call. Someone reported that their neighbor in a lower-income housing area was raising children in a filthy house. Two police officers and I headed over to investigate.

The neighborhood from which the call came wasn't that bad. Some houses looked nicer than others; some people had taken care of their lawns and driveways and gardens. Other houses were modest and worn, but not terrible. I had seen much worse neighborhoods. As we cruised down the street searching for the right address I began to wonder, "Did someone prank us? Is there really a bad situation here or was someone playing a joke on a friend?"

We found the right house, pulled up in front, and my skepticism increased. The place looked completely normal for that neighborhood. It wouldn't have won any home show awards, but it didn't stand out from other houses either. The police officers and I ran our eyes over it for a moment, looking for signs of what trouble might be inside. Finally, I shrugged. "Let's go check it out," I said, opening the car door. "Doesn't look too bad. Maybe it won't be anything."

The officers and I walked to the porch, and one of them rapped on the door with his knuckles. Their job was to stand by in case I needed backup. My job was to assess how bad the living situation was and if the children needed to be removed. From what I saw on the outside, I couldn't really envision that happening. I mentally prepared myself for a conversation with the mother, knowing I might have to be stern about some things if I saw evidence of neglect, or that I might have to apologize for the interruption if the house was in order.

A woman opened the door and a foul odor hit me like a punch in the stomach, causing me to physically recoil. Standing behind the woman were two teenage children, and behind them my eyes took in a sight almost too disgusting to believe. Dirty clothes, garbage, and piles of household items totally obscured the floor. Chairs were overturned and the couch was functioning as one large insect hotel. Thousands of bugs in varying shapes and sizes scurried openly on walls, floors, ceilings, and furniture—and on the people themselves. It was as if the insect kingdom had taken ownership of the house, and the people were just tenants.

As politely but firmly as I could, I said, "I'm Nancy Alcorn from Child Protective Services. I got a call from a neighbor about living conditions here. Do you mind if I come in and have a look around?"

It was obvious she didn't want me to come in, but with the police present she reluctantly stepped back to let me through. The police officers elected to stay on the porch.

Our polite conversation seemed almost laughable given how obviously bad their living situation was. Defying my gut, which was twisting with revulsion, I stepped in. The environment felt positively dangerous with pathogens, vermin, and almost overpowering smells.

"I'm not going to touch anything unless I have to," I thought. "There's no way I'm sitting down in this place."

The living room reminded me of a city dump with mounds of discarded stuff. As I approached the kitchen, swarms of bugs made way for me on the floor. Hundreds disappeared under the counters and into piles of dishes in the sink. I noticed that many of them scurried into the fridge itself. I opened the fridge to find food in various stages of decomposition and countless roaches and insects living among the banquet, dining at will.

"How do they even get in there?" I wondered, closing the door with an irrepressible shudder.

I stepped back carefully into the living room and made my way into the hallway. A new and more repulsive smell assaulted my nasal passages. It was so bad, so acrid that I had to will myself to move closer to the source. I followed it into a bedroom where the stench became so thick that it engulfed my other senses. There I saw a bed with a bedspread heaped on it. On the bedspread was blood and what looked like a rotting pile of yuck. The mystery substance was old enough to have dried up but was still unbelievably nasty and emanated foulness.

I pointed to the bedspread. "What is that?" I asked the mother, who had followed me.

"That's where our dog had puppies," she said.

"How long ago were the puppies born?"

"A few weeks ago."

I looked around. There were no dogs. It seemed that even the animals possessed enough sense to get out of this diseased, disgusting situation. In third world countries I had visited people in mud huts whose dwellings were organized and tidy, not overrun with vermin. In poverty there can be order and cleanliness when people make the most of what they have. But this—this was far beyond what I had seen anyplace on the planet. I didn't know it was humanly possible to survive in this kind of filth.

By now I had seen enough.

"We're pulling these kids out of here tonight," I told the mother as I walked back to the front room. "I cannot believe y'all are living like this."

I had a few other choice words for her as well, expressing my shock at how she was raising her children and caring for herself. The children walked with me to the car without complaint—they would be placed in emergency foster care. They seemed oblivious to how unsafe their home environment was. Familiarity is a powerful and blinding force.

Before getting in the car I had the police officers shine their flashlights on me, checking for bugs. Though I hadn't sat down or so much as touched a wall, roaches and other insects were crawling on my back and hair. The officers had to pick them off and toss them away. I couldn't imagine spending a single hour in that place, let alone living there, and my heart was grieved for those kids and angry at their mom. It was the most awful living situation I have ever seen.

That experience gave me a strong and graphic image of what the enemy wants to do to us. Jesus says we are the temple of the Holy Spirit (1 Cor. 6:19), but the devil is working hard to create a filthy, disgusting environment inside each of us. The devil has a vision for your life, and it's a lot worse than what I saw that night.

The "normal" lives we lead often cover up real trouble or even filth on the inside. In Jesus's day the religious leaders were the best-looking people of all. Their clothes were meticulously clean, their hands washed down to a science, their prayers super-righteous sounding. But Jesus shocked them by calling them whitewashed tombs, full of dead men's bones (Matt. 23:27). That's a pretty disgusting picture—people with lives full of stinking, rotting corpses. No wonder they couldn't stand Jesus. He shined a light on their internal ugliness.

Jesus sees reality inside and out. He knew that those men were not being transformed by God's living presence, but rather were full of death. The warnings he gave them are for us as well. You and I may look good on the outside, but are we full of rotting stuff? Is there baggage we're just not dealing with? Are we side-tracked and bothered by problems and struggles? Are our lives increasingly small and hemmed in by self-imposed limitations and things we can't overcome?

The outside of the house we visited that night gave no indication what was inside. I would have driven right by it without a thought. Yet inside was chaos and death. In the same way, if we look and act like Christians, that doesn't bother the enemy one bit. We can go to church and Bible studies and small groups for the next fifty years, but if our lives are chaotic and desperate and weak on the inside, he has reached his goal.

What baggage are you carrying around that you haven't dealt with? Perhaps you've been avoiding it for years, but it's there and it's not going away on its own.

Jesus sounded harsh, but He was not condemning those religious leaders. He was offering them freedom. He does the same with us. Only when we see the reality of who we are will we appreciate the gift of God. Indeed, the Bible says many of those leaders turned and believed (John 12:42)—and so can we.

The problem is that many people who try to be followers of Jesus only make a part-time commitment. Imagine being a part-time wife or husband. A part-time parent. A full-time worker who insits upon working only part-time hours or only coming in when it fits your schedule. None of those scenarios would work. In the same way, coming to Christ was designed by God to be a total commitment. It really doesn't work any other way. God made no plans for part-time Christians. There is no path for those who walk with Jesus some of the time and jump over to their own path whenever they feel like it.

Those who try to have a part-time relationship with God fall into several deadly traps. Let's take a look at them.

TRAP #1:
"I DON'T HAVE TO GO ALL IN"

The first trap is to treat salvation like a relationship of convenience. Lots of people see God as a buffet restaurant where you take things you like—rescue from hell, no more guilt, better friends—and leave the rest for the busboy to clean up. The Bible makes it very clear that we must go all the way with God. It's not always easy to follow Christ, but He expects a total commitment from us. We only get the benefits of walking in freedom by going all in with Him.

If you have not committed your life to Christ, now is the time to do so. The rest of this book will not work for you if you do not take this step. Consider carefully and deeply the total commitment it requires. Jesus said no general goes to war without considering first if he can win the war, and no person starts to build a tower unless he is sure he can finish it (Luke 14:28–33). He was calling people to consider the magnitude of the commitment they were making. Then He invited them to "Follow me" (Matt. 4:19).

In 2008 I was speaking at a conference hosted by a church in Hollywood, California. This church has a heart to help the down-and-out, bringing in people who have lived on the streets. While I was talking, I suddenly felt my words empowered by God. My subject was the difference between treatment and transformation and I began to say, "If you are here today and have an eating disorder or alcohol or drug addiction, you can choose freedom! It's your choice—you can be free!" When the Holy Spirit comes like a wind under your words and elevates them, it's usually because someone there needs to hear that specific message from God.

After I was done speaking, an usher brought a forty-two-year-old woman up who wanted me to pray with her. She looked rough around the edges but was also tall and naturally attractive. She was carrying a big black bag that opened from the top, like an old-time doctor's bag from house call days. I didn't realize it then, but the bag was full of drugs and drug paraphernalia.

She got right to her point.

"I've been doing drugs since I was twelve," she said, "but you said I had a choice. I can choose to be free, right?"

"Yes," I said. "It's your choice."

"Then I want to be free!" she said, shoving her black bag at me. "I don't want drugs anymore. I want to be free."

I was so happy for this woman that I literally began jumping for joy. I wanted to seize the moment because I knew God would meet her right where she was. We prayed together immediately, and I prayed for that addiction to be broken over her. That woman has been drug-free ever since. She has spoken at all of our Mercy homes in the United States and has sent me many texts since that fall day in 2008. They always say the same thing: "I'm X number of days free in Christ." At the time of this writing I received a new one from her saying, "Today I am 2,155 days a new creation in Christ. Woohoo!" It is one of the greatest miracles I have ever seen.

She later wrote me an e-mail that read:

> I met you at the September 20 Godchicks conference, in Pasadena, California. I am a 42 year old victim of sexual abuse. I was a drug addict for 30 years. I came to you (with my little black bag) to fully surrender my addictions over to Jesus Christ as my last attempt to rid myself of that hell. You prayed over me at the altar at the Church of

the Nazarene AND I HAVE NOT DONE DRUGS SINCE. I gave you my black bag that was full of paraphernalia and drugs. That was the last time I ever wanted drugs again. Jesus took it away from me. YEA!!

YOU HELPED JESUS SAVE MY LIFE AND I WILL NEVER FORGET YOU. I have you in my prayers every night and have shared my testimony with many of the people at Oasis Church in L.A.

Because of you and the Godchicks, and of course Jesus, I WILL NEVER BE THE SAME AGAIN!!!!!

Thank you so much for the powerful words you said to me that day. I am truly free. And now that I am clean from drugs, instead of hiding from the world in fear of my next relapse, I have the power and love and sound mind of Jesus Christ!

30 years I walked with the monkey on my back. NOW IT IS GONE!!!

THANK YOU THANK YOU THANK YOU

and God Bless You ALWAYS!!!

P.S. I have since started sifting through the garbage in my life, sexual abuse created. I am doing bondage breaking with 2 women at Oasis and actually have for the 1st time in my life, the hope of being a normal person, ready to be a contributing factor to God's Kingdom.

You are truly a special woman, and after God has finished making me whole, I would like to donate some time to helping you with Mercy.

I AM a child of God

Warrior Princess

Daughter of the King!!!

I was so pumped to read that! She was walking out the new life she had embraced so wholeheartedly. This woman's past life was in that black bag—and she gave it all up. Imagine the comfort and familiarity of the drugs and drug paraphernalia that had defined her existence for thirty years. Imagine the habits and lifestyle she had created in those three decades and how normal it must have seemed to her. Think of the objects she was used to handling every day, the routine she followed, the people she interacted with, the daily rhythm of her life.

Now think of the habits and patterns and stuff that defines your daily life. Would you have the courage to make such a sudden break when you saw that freedom was possible on the other side of your choice? Would you push it all away in a moment? Or would there be a tug of the familiar saying, "Stay on this path. Maybe it'll get better without changing anything"?

In a manner of speaking, each one of us has a black bag full of familiar old stuff. I'm not talking good memories and edifying habits and pictures of the grandkids. I'm talking stuff we don't need but that we have grown accustomed to. This stuff becomes such a part of our lives that we think it's normal; it's just the way we are. We know how to get along with it, and we don't want to let it go.

But when God reveals to you that something is getting in the way of your commitment to Him, it's time to let it go. Not some of it—all of it. God has given you a choice between life and death, captivity and freedom. God will honor your choice either way. Choose harmful habits and God will let you experience the results. Choose life-giving habits and God will honor your commitment just like He honored that woman's commitment and brought her onto the path of freedom.

Undoubtedly, many people reading these words have made a commitment to Christ at some point. After all, this is America and church is a big part of the culture. But just "getting saved" and baptized can be far different from being a committed follower of Christ. Think of it this way—would the people around you say that you no longer live but Christ lives in you? That was Paul's description of the Christian life in Galatians 2:20. He also wrote that Christ should be "your life" (Col. 3:4, ESV). He said he had lost everything for the sake of knowing Christ (Phil. 3:8).

Would the people around you say you had given up everything to follow Christ? Would they even know you are a Christian?

Many people I speak with wonder why they slip further into bondage and deception even though they are saved. They wonder why they still have so many life-controlling problems. In many situations it's because they made only a partial commitment to follow Christ. Total commitment leads to total freedom and clarity of purpose and vision. Partial commitment leads to further confusion.

There is no treading water in the kingdom. Jesus said, "He who is not with Me is against Me, and he who does not gather with Me scatters abroad" (Matt. 12:30). We are all moving either toward the light or toward darkness, toward greater freedom or toward bondage. The Bible calls moving in the wrong direction "drifting" (Heb. 2:1), and it often starts with the idea of partial commitment. "I'll just add Jesus to everything else I've got going," people tell themselves. "I'm sure He'll fit right in and be a useful part of my lifestyle." Jesus spoke directly to this idea when people tried to be part-time followers:

> In the same way, those of you who do not give up every-
> thing you have cannot be my disciples.
> —LUKE 14:33, NIV

Let me suggest that the amount of "death" operating in your life right now is potentially connected to your level of commitment to Christ. I'm not talking about the sufferings we sometimes undergo as believers, and I'm not doing anything silly like blaming you for your illness or for the evil someone did to you. I'm talking about areas you have not placed under the Holy Spirit's control, dark corners where something else is ruling your heart, mind, and behavior. There's truth in the old saying that if Jesus isn't Lord *of* all, He is not Lord *at* all.

Some believers think that because they appear to be living the Christian lifestyle—going to church, taking their kids (and maybe even the neighbor kids) to vacation Bible school, participating in a Bible study or small group—that they buy themselves room to overlook areas in their life they do not want to yield to God. They're still clutching that big black bag of old stuff. They have tried to make a deal with God. They might even believe they are walking in God-given freedom but find themselves entangled again and again with the same yoke of bondage (Gal. 5:1).

> So, since we're out from under the old tyranny, does that
> mean we can live any old way we want? Since we're free
> in the freedom of God, can we do anything that comes
> to mind? Hardly. You know well enough from your own
> experience that there are some acts of so-called freedom
> that destroy freedom. Offer yourselves to sin, for instance,
> and it's your last free act. But offer yourselves to the ways
> of God and the freedom never quits. All your lives you've
> let sin tell you what to do. But thank God you've started

listening to a new master, one whose commands set you free to live openly in *his* freedom!
—Romans 6:15–18, The Message

You can be an outward rule-follower, but your performance and efforts to be "good" don't by themselves indicate that your heart is right with God. We can go through the motions and appear to do the right things and still miss the heart of the gospel. Jesus said:

Many will say to Me on that day, "Lord, Lord, have we not prophesied in Your name, cast out demons in Your name, and done many wonderful works in Your name?" But then I will declare to them, "I never knew you. Depart from Me, you who practice evil."
—Matthew 7:22–23

Years ago when I worked at a correctional facility for teenage girls, the only person on that campus who was allowed to bring up spiritual things in an official capacity was the chaplain. But guess what? Though he dressed like a chaplain and had a bunch of degrees from seminaries, he knew little or nothing about how the gospel transforms lives. He didn't really believe. When girls would ask about the possibility of experiencing freedom by doing what Jesus said to do and applying the gospel in their personal lives, he would say, "Why don't you talk to Nancy about that? She probably knows the answer."

Here I was, a Christian working there as the athletic director of the facilities, and even though I was very young, the chaplain was referring girls to me because he couldn't answer their spiritual questions! How did that happen? I hope it was because he could see that I had a relationship with Christ and was totally committed—not perfect, but totally committed. It makes a big difference.

Anyone can wear the religious uniform, have the clerical collar, put the Bible under his arm, and listen to praise and worship music at work. I've known a number of people like that chaplain who looked like Christians and were paid to be spiritual leaders—and they didn't even believe in the transforming power of the gospel. It's not the look; it's what's inside. And when people try to go part-time with God, the inside stays really messy.

Are you all in for God? Or are you holding back? Remember, "Once you were dead because of your disobedience and your many sins. You used to live in sin, just like the rest of the world, obeying the devil—the commander of the powers in the unseen world. He is the spirit at work in the hearts of those who refuse to obey God. All of us used to live that way, following the passionate desires and inclinations of our sinful nature. By our very nature we were subject to God's anger, just like everyone else" (Eph. 2:1–3, NLT). But now we are to "live as people who are free, not using your freedom as a cover-up for evil, but living as servants of God" (1 Pet. 2:16, ESV).

God gives grace to the humble (James 4:6, 1 Pet. 5:5), and it takes humility to admit we've been just partially committed and need to give ourselves entirely to Christ. But if you have a life-controlling problem you're going to need that grace. The Bible tells us:

> There is no one righteous, not even one.
> —ROMANS 3:10, NIV

> For all have sinned and come short of the glory of God.
> —ROMANS 3:23

> For the wages of sin is death.
> —ROMANS 6:23

> There is a way that appears to be right, but in the end it
> leads to death.
> —Proverbs 14:12, niv

In this book we will talk about many components of freedom. You may even take them in a different sequence. But I am convinced it all starts with the choice to commit totally to Christ. Not part-time, not halfway. Totally. Fully. All in.

If you are rededicating your life I want to point you to three scriptures I think are important. Proverbs 24:16 says, "For the righteous falls seven times and rises again, but the wicked stumble in times of calamity" (esv).

That may be you. You can be righteous and still fall. The proof of your commitment is that you rise. Micah 7:8 affirms the same truth when it says, "Do not rejoice over me, my enemy! Although I have fallen, I will rise." Acts 3:19 says, "Repent, then, and turn to God, so that your sins may be wiped out, that times of refreshing may come from the Lord" (niv).

There is always room for repentance in God's plan. If you made a strong commitment at one point but drifted away, come back now. The righteous rise! That's you!

Trap #2:
"I Need to Clean Up My Life."

When we commit to Christ we get the most unbelievable deal in the universe. Jesus takes our sin and filthy rags and gives us His righteousness (2 Cor. 5:21). You won't find a better exchange than that. Not only does He give you the best life now but He gives you eternal life with Him. And we didn't do a thing to deserve it!

For some people, that's the obstacle. They find it hard to accept God's gift as free. It's so opposite of the human system that gives us only what we earn and deserve. If any of the following statements describe your viewpoint, you may have a hard time making that total commitment:

- ❀ "I'll accept God's gift of salvation, but there are some areas I want to clean up first. I know I can do better. Then I'll add God to my life."

- ❀ "I don't really deserve God's mercy so after I get saved I'll just keep working to earn it as I try to hit that high standard."

- ❀ "I don't want to fully commit because I know I won't be able to do it perfectly. Why lie to God about keeping up my end of the bargain?"

- ❀ "I have a couple of habits I don't want to bring into my relationship with God, and I feel like He's waiting on me to get control of them before I get on board with Him."

Those are lies. Jesus's message is, "Come as you are" (see John 7:37 and Luke 18:13). If that offends your pride—good. The sooner you get rid of your pride, the sooner you'll see through the confusion and connect with reality. Jesus said, "Come to me, all you who are weary and burdened, and I will give you rest" (Matt. 11:28, NIV). Not, "Get your act together first and then remain perfect and I'll give you rest." My friend, we get the best deal the world has ever seen. Second Corinthians 5:21 describes it this way: "God made Him who knew no sin to be sin for us, that we might become the righteousness of God in Him." Our future as believers is unbelievably hopeful and bright.

As a young Christian, I had a hard time switching gears from my worldly mentality and accepting that Jesus welcomed me even though I wasn't good enough. It was hard for me to rest on His goodness and not my own. In that same chapter in 2 Corinthians

Paul talks about God putting robes of righteousness on us in exchange for our old, yucky clothes. I'm a visual person so sometimes I would picture myself wearing a nasty, tattered robe with holes and spots all over it. Then I'd imagine Jesus coming and taking that ugly thing and putting on me this beautiful, white, plush robe, the kind they have in fancy hotels. The contrast would be almost too much for me to accept. I found it so hard to understand why He would take all our mistakes and declare us not guilty before the Father. I couldn't handle that Jesus stands next to us with pride before the Father, and we appear pure and clean—without earning a bit of it.

Maybe you're like me and the judgment of God is a lot easier to accept than His mercy. Judgment makes sense to us and mercy doesn't. Judgment fits into our human logic. I knew how dirty I was. I knew the deal Jesus was getting when He got me. Before I was saved I even behaved worse when I felt God wooing me. I tried to resist His grace. The girl who kept talking to me about God and inviting me to church was so annoying and persistent in her love and patience that I tried to drive her away by using profanity around her and talking about drinking and partying the weekend before. My goal was to push her away with my worst attributes.

I didn't know that you can't push away real love. My swearing and boasting didn't change anything. She kept loving me with a force I couldn't resist. When I finally couldn't stand it any longer I called her and agreed to attend a church youth group meeting where a lot of high school and college students were sharing powerful testimonies of their transformed lives. Hearing their testimonies changed my life, and I made a decision for Christ as a result.

But it took a while for me to love mercy as much as I had loved judgment. When I did, I felt liberated at a deep level. I was one of the many weary and burdened ones who found rest in Jesus. God has chosen to show mercy to people. We don't have a choice in the matter. We will never be good enough to deserve it. The only thing you can do is let go of your pride and say yes.

TRAP #3:
"I DIDN'T FEEL ANYTHING. AM I REALLY SAVED?"

Other people think, "I gave my life to Christ, but I didn't really feel anything so I'm pretty sure it didn't work." That's a trap I narrowly avoided. On August 9, 1972, I gave my heart to Christ, but I didn't feel much in my emotions at that moment. After saying the prayer I looked at the people gathered around praying with me and said, "Is that it? Did I get saved? Shouldn't I have seen some bolt of lightning or heard thunder? Are y'all sure this worked? Am I a Christian now?" One of them quoted 1 John 1:9, which says, "If we confess our sins, He is faithful and just to forgive us our sins and cleanse us from all unrighteousness."

"Do you believe this is the Word of God?" she asked me.

I thought about it for a moment—yeah, I did believe that. Then it clicked: we weren't going by feelings anymore. The Word is God's truth and light. It is permanent and unchanging. It is true no matter how I feel about it. My salvation was a done deal. It's not about how I feel; it's something I receive by faith. That one realization has given me more stability in times of turmoil than perhaps any other. I know it will do the same for you.

I can promise you now, you won't feel "saved" every day, or even every week. But settle it in your heart that your status before God does not change according to whichever emotions you woke up with yesterday morning. Jesus is the same yesterday, today, and forever (Heb. 13:8). Your emotions will go up and down. He will be your constant.

Trap #4:
"I Tried God and It Didn't Work for Me."

Some people come into relationship with God and want to define the terms, set the schedule, give Him their list of goals, and pretty much decide how it's going to work. When those expectations are not met they say, "I guess being a Christian isn't for me. God let me down."

Here's a little news: God is not going to jump on your agenda and give you everything on your wish list. He is not your cosmic servant or genie from a bottle. He has a plan for your life, and He likes His plan better than yours. You will too—eventually.

Sometimes when people commit their lives to Christ they want to see big changes in all areas of life right away. Big changes do happen, but many changes take time. God's plan is His process. The Bible talks about working out our salvation by "faith and patience" (Heb. 6:12). The best things take time. A baby laid in a feeding trough took thirty years to grow into the Savior of the world. A mustard seed planted in the ground takes months and years to grow into a large bush that provides homes for the birds. The Bible says not to despise small beginnings (Zech. 4:10). If you want big things with God, you have to be OK starting with very little ones.

Is it possible you are frustrated, looking for major changes and improvements in your life when God is drawing your attention to little things right around you? Are you obeying His voice by being more patient with people at work? Kinder to people in everyday interactions? Spending more time with Him in prayer and the Word? If not, how can you move on to bigger and better things? He is waiting for you to be faithful with little things.

God has been patient with us so let's not get impatient with Him. God calls Himself "the author and finisher of our faith"

(Heb. 12:2). Your first step of faith may be simply to rest in Him. Dial down. Chill. He started the relationship and He's in the lead. "He who has begun a good work in you will complete it until the day of Jesus Christ" (Phil. 1:6, NKJV).

In the Gospel of John, some of Jesus's followers got hyped up about doing the same works that Jesus was doing (John 6:28). They wanted to perform big miracles, so they asked Jesus how. He said, and this is a Nancy Alcorn paraphrase, "Don't worry about that yet. Your first job is to believe in me. Relax. Don't get ahead of yourself. Let's start by walking together and having a relationship. Your faith will grow into bigger stuff at the right time." (See John 6:29.)

Follow His lead and let it work in small and quiet ways, because eventually His work in you will grow so large that you never saw it coming.

TRAP #5:
"I WASN'T THAT BAD BEFORE.
I'VE SORT OF ALWAYS BEEN A CHRISTIAN."

Those who grew up in good Christian homes and an atmosphere of belief are some of the luckiest people I know—and, at times, the most complacent. I want to rattle their cages and say, "Don't you know what you got saved from? You weren't perfect before— you were going to hell like the rest of us. Wake up! Salvation is a big deal!"

When people think they have "always been saved" they can go through life with no real expectation or knowledge of what God can do. They live on slow speed with no urgency in their purpose and goals. They might even have a hard time seeing how God has worked in their lives. His activity and wonderful help might seem invisible to them.

At Mercy homes we have girls write out their life stories so they can see how God has interacted with them in the past. Some write it like a short story. Some create a visual timeline with significant events. Some make collages out of colorful images clipped from magazines. In each case the point is to find God in their stories, to start thinking about the past from His perspective, and to see how He was working in their lives even when they were unaware of Him.

One of my favorite salvation stories is from a friend of mine who was not raised in church. As a girl she discovered *The Chronicles of Narnia* by C. S. Lewis. She was drawn to the character Aslan, and when Aslan chose to die for a disobedient boy named Edmund, my friend thought, "That's amazing. That's the greatest thing ever." Her heart was knit with this fictional character. When life went wacky around her, she thought of Aslan's example. She had undying trust that even if people made strange and hurtful decisions, Aslan was always true. He always did the right thing. Aslan gave her an internal stability and a glimpse of real goodness. She would think of Aslan and say, "You're amazing. Other people are crazy, but you're amazing."

When she was seventeen someone talked to her about Jesus. She immediately recognized her childhood hero, Aslan, in the personality of this man from Galilee. She thought, "I know exactly who Jesus is—He's Aslan. And He died for me? And He's faithful and good even when people around Him act crazy? And He's really real? I'm all in."

This friend of mine was a popular girl and a cheerleader, but she threw her whole life into Christ. She made a very public declaration of commitment to let her friends know this was her defining day. Years later when she was in her thirties, God spoke to her one day during prayer and said, "I specifically spoke the gospel through the Narnia books to you. I was watching you that whole time and made sure you saw those books and read them." She calls C. S. Lewis her "childhood pastor."

Reflect for a moment on the journey that brought you to Christ. Why did you give your life to Christ? What kind of commitment did you make to Him? Did you say any words that were significant to you? Did He say anything significant to you? What did you expect salvation to mean for your future? Maybe you have a sweet and wonderful story of God wooing you from childhood like my friend does. Maybe, like me, you resisted for a long time and finally saw your need. There are a thousand different experiences and ways that people come to Christ. But I'm convinced He's at work in our lives long before we know it. The Bible says, "But God demonstrates His own love toward us, in that while we were yet sinners, Christ died for us" (Rom. 5:8). That means he had a plan to purchase salvation for every person before He even went to the cross. It's mind-boggling yet true. Our job is to receive the salvation He paid for on that cross.

For myself, I still find it amazing that God seeks us. Consider for a moment whom we are dealing with. This is not some needy deity begging for a relationship with us out of some lack or need of His own. This is the Creator of the world, the One who made everything you see and knew you before you were in your mother's womb. We should be the ones begging for relationship with this incredibly fascinating, beautiful, powerful God. And yet He takes the first step toward us. Incredible!

> "What man among you having a hundred sheep and losing one of them does not leave the ninety-nine in the wilderness and go after the one which is lost until he finds it? And when he has found it, he places it on his shoulders, rejoicing."
>
> —Luke 15:4–5

But God is so rich in mercy, and he loved us so much, that even though we were dead because of our sins, he gave us life when he raised Christ from the dead....God saved you by his grace when you believed. And you can't take credit for this; it is a gift from God. Salvation is not a reward for the good things we have done, so none of us can boast about it. For we are God's masterpiece. He has created us anew in Christ Jesus, so we can do the good things he planned for us long ago.

—EPHESIANS 2:4–5, 8–10, NLT

Therefore, since we have been justified by faith, we have peace with God through our Lord Jesus Christ.

—ROMANS 5:1

For I will forgive their wickedness and will remember their sins no more.

—HEBREWS 8:12, NIV

Come now, and let us reason together, says the LORD. Though your sins be as scarlet, they shall be as white as snow; though they be red like crimson, they shall be as wool.

—ISAIAH 1:18

As far as the east is from the west, so far has He removed our transgressions from us.

—PSALM 103:12

If salvation feels like no big deal to you, may I suggest you need to get in touch with reality. If you think God got a good catch when you came to Him, then you've got it backward. That thinking will stunt your growth in Christ and keep you in bondage to apathy and smugness, not to mention the fact that it will lead to a lack of gratitude, lack of humility, and lack of love.

Jesus told a Pharisee that one who is forgiven much loves much. Maybe it's time to look again at how much God forgave you, to help you love more.

Salvation is a massive deal. It should touch our emotions every day that we are no longer heading to hell and living in confusion, darkness, and total futility. Total commitment to Christ means celebrating every day we are alive and letting it wash away our pride, self-sufficiency, and ingratitude.

TRAP #6:
"YOU WILL ALWAYS HAVE YOUR PROBLEM, EVEN IF YOU FOLLOW JESUS."

As much good as the medical and mental health industries do, in many cases medications are actually being used to mask the symptoms instead of getting to the root of the problem. The real question is not whether psychotropic medications are helpful or harmful; the question is whether or not they are actually necessary in every case. Over the years, we have had hundreds of girls walk through the doors of Mercy in a heavily medicated state after being in various treatment programs and psychiatric hospitals. I am all for treating people with medications when they actually need it, but at Mercy we have found that the medications can actually mask the pain of the underlying issues.

The girls who enter our program at Mercy struggle with issues such as bitterness, resentment, unforgiveness, and all kinds of trauma resulting from rape, sexual abuse, sex trafficking, extreme neglect, and other causes. Thankfully, we work with medical doctors and psychiatrists who understand the spiritual aspect of what we do at Mercy as we help these girls work through the issues. We have found that once we are able to take the girls through the counseling process and they begin to find freedom and healing, these doctors are often able to decrease their medications. In some cases, the medications are greatly reduced, and in others, the girls no longer need any medication at all by the time they graduate from the Mercy program.

For example, Nicky came to Mercy after being in forty-three different hospitals and group homes. She had been hospitalized more than a hundred times. When Nicky came into the program, she was on eight strong psychotropic drugs and taking twelve pills a day. By the time she graduated from Mercy, the doctors felt like Nicky still needed to be on four medications, but they were able to significantly reduce the dosage of those medications. Within eight months after graduating from Mercy, Nicky was able to come off all medications. If Nicky had never worked through her issues at Mercy, she would still be living in that same drug-induced state in which she entered the program due to overmedication. Instead, Nicky graduated from Mercy in February 2013, at which time she entered a yearlong program that trains individuals for overseas missionary work. She then went on to do three weeks of mission work in various locations in Central Asia. Nicky is now a healthy and whole young woman who has a passion for serving God and people!

We always make sure to tell girls like Nicky that someone who has a chemical imbalance and needs medication should not feel that she is damaged goods or flawed. It is no different from someone who has to take a sinus pill or medicine for high blood pressure. The goal is not to be off all medications. Instead, the goal is to be off all medications that are not necessary.

Lisa came to Mercy in 1999 at the age of seventeen. She had been told that she would have to go into a long-term psychiatric facility for the rest of her life. Lisa's parents decided to give her an opportunity to come to Mercy to see if we could help her. She was on seven different medications when she came to Mercy, including anti-anxiety, anti-depression, and anti-seizure medications for mood stabilization. The medications Lisa was taking were so strong that none of the doctors in Nashville would even see her. We had to fly Lisa back home to Houston on a monthly basis to have her medications evaluated by her psychiatrist.

The average length of stay for a girl at Mercy is six months, but because of the trauma in her background, it took Lisa nine months to graduate from the program. During those nine months Lisa worked through her issues and was able to get off of every single one of the heavy drugs she had been taking. Since leaving Mercy, Lisa no longer requires any medication at all. She is happily married to a wonderful man, and they have three beautiful children. Lisa spent some time on staff at a megachurch in the Houston area, and today she is a stay-at-home mom and still actively involved in her local church. The healing and freedom Lisa found allowed her to come off every medication she had been taking!

It is common in many treatment programs and psychiatric wards to use the term "recovering" addict, "recovering" alcoholic, "recovering" from depression, or whatever the issue is. The problem with that terminology is that it keeps you tied to your past and continually identifying with the issue from which you have been freed. It encourages you to walk in a victim mentality by implying that you are still in bondage to your issues and unable to walk in complete freedom.

At Mercy we are not about treatment; we are about transformation. The Bible teaches us in 2 Corinthians 5:17 that if anyone receives Christ, they are "a new creation; old things have passed away; behold, all things have become new" (NKJV). The old person we used to be is dead and gone, and we now start a new life with a new beginning, no longer identifying with our past. We are all aware that we have a past, but we do not have to allow our past to destroy our future. We can move forward in our new identity as a child of God—forgiven and free!

The apostle Paul described himself in the Bible as the "worst" of sinners (1 Tim. 1:15). However, in Philippians 3:13, Paul said that he may not be all he should be yet, but "one thing I do, forgetting those things which are behind and reaching forward to those things which are ahead." Enough said!

TRAP #7:
"I'LL CALL ON GOD WHEN I NEED HIM."

Years before she worked at Mercy, Mary had fallen through the cracks of society and found herself in a dark world of addiction. Her life didn't look different from any other young woman with a church background from a middle-class family navigating her way through growing up. However, the enemy knew her weakness, and what started as Mary experimenting with drugs and alcohol simply trying to fit in, soon spiraled into full-blown addictions.

Three years into Mary's drug and alcohol addictions she had sold or lost everything that meant anything to her and still didn't have enough money to keep up her habits. She decided that all she had left to sell was her body. She tried to kill herself, but someone found her in time to save her. That made her even angrier at God— He wouldn't even let her die.

After six years in a haze of substance abuse and prostitution she realized she could not go on. She couldn't get enough drugs, alcohol, or sex to drown out the pain and anger she had stored up, and she didn't have the strength to keep up that lifestyle any longer. The thought of giving her life back to God at that time was almost as miserable to her as continuing on. When she did turn to Him it wasn't with tears of repentance but in anger and defeat.

She knew she couldn't make it without Him, so she threw her life at Him and dared Him to do something better with it.

He took the offer.

Soon, Mary was back home and going through withdrawals. She chose to withdraw from drugs without professional support, a decision she says she wouldn't repeat. She would wobble into the kitchen of her parents' home holding on to the counter so she wouldn't fall down. Her body would tremble badly, and her tongue would feel thick. A number of times her father stood behind her and her mother in front, locking their arms around her and praying while she convulsed. God's grace brought her through that time but the confusion didn't immediately subside. She spent a year trying to stabilize, and there were times of loneliness that drove her back to old friends and drugs. Sometimes she would give in to an old lover and return to her parents' house wearing a familiar shame. But God kept loving her and showing her that she didn't have to go backward to move ahead in life.

One day Mary simply decided that no matter what happened she would not go back to anything or anyone from her past. She pictured her old life on one side of a divide and her new life on the other. She knew that if she ever crossed into her old life again she would not find her way back. At the next worship service at church the words of the songs touched her deeply and she wept for a long time. God began to wash away her pain, and Mary learned that every time she remembered something painful, she could lift it up with her hands in worship or prayer and God would take her brokenness like an offering.

Mary's decision to recommit her life to Christ led to a total turnaround. She served as a key leader on our staff at Mercy for more than fourteen years and helped other young women find freedom. She has since moved on to another ministry with the same heart to bring freedom to those in captivity.

What strikes me most about Mary's story is that before the drugs took over her life, she didn't look any different from what I looked like as a young woman. Indeed, we all look pretty much the same until temptations and trials swoop in to test us. Jesus likened it to building a house (Matt. 7:24–29). You can take time to dig down and lay the proper foundation, or you can carelessly and quickly build on sand. Both houses look good...for a while. Then both get battered by wind, waves, and rain. The quality of your commitment and foundation are tested in those storms. Many people live in houses built on sand; it's just that nobody knows until they collapse.

The point I'm making is that choosing total commitment to Christ now will guard your freedom in the future. Every one of us is tried and tested in this life. You don't know when that next test or temptation will arrive. When it does, partial commitment to Jesus isn't going to do much for you. It's like physical health. Viruses and bacteria are always in our environment trying to take advantage of weakness in our immune systems. When we are well rested and healthy, our immune systems withstand those attacks mostly without our even knowing it.

But when we run ourselves down and weaken our immune systems, those invaders can get a foothold. Part-time commitment to Christ is like that—a weakened immune system, a poor foundation, exposure to danger. Total commitment will give you great stability when difficulties come to test your character. You may not even realize you were under attack. Jesus slept through a storm until His disciples woke Him up. (See Matthew 8:23-27.) You can have that same peace if you lay the right foundation ahead of time. When the storms arrive to batter your house, it will be too late to build anymore, and the quality of your life will be exposed.

Let's end this chapter by making a prayer of commitment or recommitment. I believe in you just as Jesus believes in you.

I know He has a purpose and plan for you that will completely amaze you. It starts each day with making a total commitment to Him. Let's pray:

> *Lord, I love You. Nobody has ever done more for me than You, and nobody ever will. You deserve my total trust and commitment, and I offer it to You now with a sincere heart. Help me to lay that strong foundation and to walk in the freedom and benefits of a total commitment to You. Thank You for totally committing to me even when I didn't care about You and didn't know who You were. Thank You for giving Your life in hope of having a relationship with me one day. I commit to our relationship now. Amen.*

Chapter 2

KEY #2: HEALING LIFE'S HURTS

Cissy was looking forward to rafting the Ocoee River in Chattanooga with her church group. The section of river they were going to travel included a man-made course set up for competition in the 1996 Atlanta Olympics. This course included class four and five rapids, which sounded pretty intense, but with her athletic background Cissy felt she could handle it. The guides reassured everyone that even beginners could go safely through the difficult section.

Cissy boarded the bus at church and headed into nature for what she expected to be a wonderful adventure with friends surrounded by glorious scenery. They arrived at the river and Cissy noticed that her raft-mates were all women except for one man, and most of the women were not very fit. Her guide was a woman too. Cissy felt a little nervous about that and wished there were a little more strength in case something went wrong. But nobody else seemed to notice so she went along.

Calm waters welcomed them for the first few miles. The breeze was nice; the sun dappled the river's surface through overhanging leaves. It couldn't have been a lovelier day. The conversation and company were nice. Then they entered the Olympic course, and a coldness set in. The river became boisterous, the waters loud, the peaceful day suddenly tense and dark.

"Row! Push!" the guide yelled as their raft plunged into the rapids, but Cissy could barely hear her above the roar of the water. The raft began shifting and turning in disconcerting ways.

They hit a particular rapid called Humongous and went sideways. Cissy's side of the raft bucked up and came down, hurling Cissy out backward. She found herself under the raft and in a whirlpool with the raft on top of her. The raft pushed on her head and kept her under. She pushed on it with her arms but couldn't make it budge. Someone thrust an oar into the water but she didn't see it. She was taking water in fast. "This might be the end," she thought.

It seemed to her that the waters had actually attacked her and dragged her into the treacherous current. Now, as Cissy was trapped under the boat, the river shoved its way down her throat. Cissy became aware of a spiritual reality she had not sensed before—the dangerous situation seemed part of the enemy's plan to take her out. She felt he was purposefully trying to drown her.

Suddenly a current pushed her out from under the boat and she flew down the river at the mercy of the waves. Full of dread, she could barely thrust her head above water to grab a breath. The safety vest did little against the tons of pounding water. Tumbling as if in a violent washing machine, Cissy found herself caught between life and death. The enemy felt near yet God felt nearer. Cissy was not afraid of dying because she knew she would go to heaven. But the spiritual tug of war was maddening. Over and over she rolled in the rapids, praying for the struggle to end. Battle raged over her soul, the enemy trying to pummel her to death and drown her and God fighting to save her. For the first minute or two, guides in other rafts threw ropes toward her and yelled at her to grab on.

Every attempt failed. Then Cissy was pulled downriver beyond the rafts. Nobody was there. The river's roar filled her ears.

Over and over the wall of water slammed her against rocks and boulders. "Is this the way it's going to end?" she thought. "Is this really how I die? I just can't believe it." The rocks beat her body like metal on an anvil, remorselessly. Her left hip and leg screamed for it to stop. Then for a moment the rapids flattened out and the river ceased its anger. Cissy was able to turn onto her back and float. At that moment, with no more strength left, she gave up the fight, closed her eyes, and surrendered to the outcome. She felt God undergird her and His face shine down on her like the sun. However it ended—even if there were more rapids ahead and she did not survive—she was at peace. She lay there glad to be alive but ready for death. "Take me now, Lord," she prayed. "I'm all right."

There was a noise. A safety boat had caught up and was trying to get ahead of her. It pulled downriver and Cissy's body ran into it. She knew it was God's salvation in action as the men lifted her from the water and lay her in the boat. As relieved as she was to be safe, her mind still reeled in the timeless struggle she had just endured. The guides talked to her but Cissy did not respond. A good friend of hers was in the boat with them and kept looking at her with evident concern. Cissy's left leg was swollen to twice its size from all the hits and her shoe had been torn off. Thankfully, she had suffered no cuts or gashes.

After a good half hour of being in shock, Cissy felt her head clear and she began doing what she always did: making jokes to put everyone at ease. In her family, nobody was encouraged to ask for help, and Cissy wasn't very good about expressing her needs. The guides and support people did not offer medical support and Cissy didn't ask to go to a hospital. She hoped that someone would try to get some care for her leg but when they didn't she acted like it was no big deal. Nobody in her church group even stopped to pray for her. A different group from another church heard about her accident and prayed for her before they all left the river. But when Cissy got on the bus to go home she was in so much physical and emotional pain she could hardly stand it. She sat at the back of bus, covered her head so no one could see her, and cried.

At home she was a mess. She could hardly drink water because it made her sick to think of taking in more water, as she had when nearly drowning. Lying in bed she had flashbacks and nightmares of drowning and would wake up gasping for air. When she tried to go to the bathroom she couldn't get out of bed. The muscles in her stomach felt like they had done a thousand crunches. Her body was so tight from fighting against the water that she had to roll out of bed and onto the floor just to get to the bathroom.

Still reluctant to ask for help or admit there was a problem, Cissy kept coming to work and living as normally as she could. But the first time she watched a movie where someone got pulled under water, she had to walk out of the room. And the nightmares continued. She would wake up feeling like she was drowning.

She also noticed she was irritable and distant. When her friends talked about TV shows and what they'd read in the latest magazine, Cissy would get upset. "Who cares about those things?" she would think. "Talk about things that matter." She felt that most conversations were trivial and meaningless. Her formerly upbeat, humorous personality became sober and serious. Everything was now about life and death. She felt isolated, lonely, and unable to relate to others in casual conversation. Joy had gone out of her life.

Bitterness, too, had put down roots. She was upset at the church workers and the river guides for their perceived lack of support. Though Cissy had not asked for help, she was angry with them for not offering it. As a counselor by training, Cissy knew the damage unforgiveness could do so she made a conscious choice to forgive everyone who had been there that day—friends, guides, the bus driver, the leaders of her group. She discovered that forgiveness is a daily habit. Anytime she saw people who had been on the river trip she had to forgive them all over again for acting like nothing had happened.

But forgiveness alone wasn't enough. Her mind still struggled with the incident. She was tired from lack of sleep and normal life was getting difficult. One day after counseling others at work Cissy thought, "I need to take time to pray through the hurts from this rafting incident. I need to get well."

She sat down on her couch and said, "OK, God, let's do this." She couldn't forgive a river, but she could pray through the entire experience, inviting Him into her memory of it. She closed her eyes and let her mind go back to what had happened. "Lord, I'm under water in this struggle," she said, narrating the memory as it played through her mind. At the moment she back-flipped out of the boat she invited God into the memory and asked Him to show Himself to her in what was happening.

Cissy saw herself under water, but she also saw something new in her mind's eye: a light was wrapped around her. The light stayed with her throughout the experience and made her feel protected and safe. She kept proceeding through the memory, seeing herself flying downriver and about to drown. In that memory she now saw something new—God's hand in the water with her, sustaining her, helping her to get back to the surface. It really had been a tug of war for her soul. One hand, a dark, cold one, was pulling her down into the river. Another, God's hand, was pulling her up. She knew that God was showing her what had happened that day.

She came to the end and realized that God had saved her for a reason. She was alive to fulfill His plan for her. Reliving the event was emotional, but Cissy stopped having nightmares from that point on. God also restored her gladness and gave her laughter again. She began reconnecting with friends. Knowing that God had fought for her made her deeply grateful and confident in His goodness and her safety in Him.

Her hip took time to heal and there were still mental hurdles to overcome. The first time she swam underwater in a pool she felt a rush of fear. It took time to get comfortable in the water again. But Cissy wasn't content just to be comfortable. She wanted to face her fears. She had gone through some counseling with a Christian counselor about the experience and felt ready to go rafting again. Cissy had learned in graduate school about methods of desensitization. You bring the thing you fear close to you and get used to having it nearby so that you no longer fear it. She started by searching online for videos of people rafting over Humongous, the rapid that had put her in the water. She listened to the sound of the rapids on the Ocoee River. Then she specifically watched videos of people flying out of their rafts and into the water. While watching it she would imagine the sights and smells of that day.

Two summers later she and some supportive and strong guy friends went to the Ocoee River to raft part of it again. Cissy was nervous. The night before their trip she walked down to the river and put her feet in, touching the rocks and absorbing the surroundings. The next day her raft partners surrounded her in prayer and promised to give her the best protection they could.

On the calm sections of the river Cissy made sure to enjoy the nature that was around them, to admire what God created. When they reached the level four rapids, Cissy was mentally ready. Their raft coasted through without incident. Cissy felt she had closed the circle for good.

She now has pictures on her wall of her first trip to the Ocoee. Someone in another raft actually took a shot of her after she had fallen into the water and was reaching for the oar. That shot hangs next to a photo of her victorious return trip where she made it down without incident.

A day that brought extreme pain ultimately gave Cissy a revelation of God's salvation in action. Cissy says the experience was very significant to her growth and helped her reach a level of maturity where she understands her place in God's plan.

HURTS FROM THE PAST

Every one of us suffers experiences that hurt us. When those hurts remain unhealed, they cause us to shrink back from life, to operate out of fear and to build our lives around avoiding more hurts. We take fewer healthy risks in relationships, jobs, and ministry. Some people even sabotage relationships because they don't think they deserve it because of the way they have been hurt in the past. Some people hurt by abandonment or loss will cling to others in their marriages or relationships, or accuse those around them of not being faithful enough. We see many examples of this at Mercy. Any person who has a deep hurt will find their decision making affected. It all springs from unhealed wounds.

The devil's plan is to use your hurts to hold you back. He wants to put boundaries on your life based on your fear of getting hurt again. Total freedom means no longer allowing hurts to direct our lives, tarnish our relationships, and shape our personalities.

After a pro-life rally in Nashville, my friend David Will and his family were eating at a restaurant. A woman there who had heard David and his wife, Lisa, speak sent them an anonymous note on a napkin:

> "I don't want to approach you. I was at the benefit for Mercy and was very blessed by the concert. I enjoyed it very much. Four years ago I was in a crisis pregnancy with nowhere to turn. The pressure to choose abortion was very great. I could not find the courage to tell my family, and I was not married. I went to a clinic of Planned Parenthood. They said abortion was the solution. However, they did not tell me the kind of hell I would live in because of my choice. I am a Christian and was a Christian at the time I made that choice. It has taken me a long time to forgive and let go. In the past six months God has begun to heal me from those scars. He's still healing me today. Your ministry is a wonderful outreach to a hurting world. I appreciate what you do. In His name. God bless you. Thanks!"*

This woman had let hurt paralyze her for several years. Thankfully, she found the path to freedom again.

Many people don't want to acknowledge their hurts because of the painful emotions attached to them. Instead of running to God with their hurts, they run away from Him to hide. For Vicky, that running was literal. Vicky suffered sexual abuse as a girl, and her abusers promised her candy and money not to tell anyone. Vicky told her parents what was happening, but they did not believe her and did not intervene. Vicky thought she wasn't good enough to save, that her life was worthless. She went to church but the things happening in her personal life left her feeling far from peaceful.

---

* From Nancy Alcorn, *Echoes of Mercy* (Lake Mary, FL: Charisma House, 2013), 230–231.

When she was still in elementary school her family moved and the abuse stopped, but it took a while for Vicky to process through the emotional devastation—and she did it on her own, thinking that nobody had experienced what she had experienced. Her way of dealing with it was to run. She was good at running. She had always been athletic and strong, climbing trees and playing sports. Now she used that gift to try to treat her emotional wounds. Whenever she felt too stressed out at home, Vicky would walk to school and start running the track. She felt a release of anger and frustration in the exertion. Whenever she felt pain from her many hurts, she "ran it out." It felt good to control something in her life, to numb out and escape reality. She was so well conditioned that she could run for a long time, sometimes to the point of exhaustion. When she stopped running, the anger that had been inside her seemed gone and she could go home.

In her senior year of high school Vicky blew out her knee and couldn't run for a while. She worked hard to get back to form and tried running in a brace, but the pain was too great to continue. During her recovery she realized she had buried herself in sports and that her priorities were out of balance. She was running away from her hurts instead of toward them. Eventually, through a number of trials, she learned that you can't run from your hurts because they always catch up. The only safe place to run is into the Father's arms.

If you're like Vicky, the idea of facing your feelings from hurts isn't very attractive. Some people conclude that because they have been so hurt, no emotions can be trusted. They won't even allow themselves to feel happiness or joy because it makes them feel out of control. The idea of going back to past hurts means unlocking the box with all the emotions in it—a dangerous and scary idea.

Debbie Harvie, who works at our Mercy home in the United Kingdom, says that overcoming her own hurts was frightening because she had to surrender protective habits to God. "It can be quite frightening to surrender them because you don't know what's on the other side," she told me.

But pouring out those emotions to God is where healing must begin. I encourage people to consider doing this with a Christian counselor if they feel it's appropriate for their situation. The fact is that God wants to hear our complaints and petitions to Him. In fact, Psalm 142:1–2 says, "I cry out to the LORD; I plead for the LORD's mercy. I pour out my complaints before him and tell him all my troubles" (NLT). He likes our honesty. When we keep our emotions inside, we can't grow in intimacy with Him. He is the only one who can bear our hurts and help us to heal. But He won't force us to be healed; He waits for us to invite Him.

While we don't base our choices on emotions, God does give us emotions to enjoy. Some emotions are meant to signal that something is going on inside of us that needs to be addressed. God Himself has emotions. Jesus experienced the whole range of human emotions during His earthly life. He was moved by compassion to heal and teach people (Matt. 14:14). He burned with anger at hard-hearted religious people (Mark 3:5). He rejoiced openly, wept openly, and loved openly (Luke 10:21, John 11:35, and Mark 10:21).

The Bible promises that "we do not have a High Priest who cannot sympathize with our weaknesses, but One who was in every sense tempted like we are, yet without sin. Let us then come with confidence to the throne of grace, that we may obtain mercy and find grace to help in time of need" (Heb. 4:15–16). Jesus sympathizes with every weakness we have. Isaiah 61:3 says He wants to give us "beauty for ashes, the oil of joy for mourning, the garment of praise for the spirit of heaviness." Jesus came to heal the brokenhearted, those stuck in emotional hurt. "But he was wounded for our transgressions, he was bruised for our iniquities; the chastisement of our peace was upon him, and by his stripes we are healed" (Isa. 53:5). That healing includes hurts from the past.

Vulnerability may seem risky, but with God there is safety. "He will cover you with his feathers, and under his wings you can hide. His truth will be your shield and protection," Psalm 91:4 tells us (NCV). You can relax knowing that God is trustworthy. He will never hurt you. He wants to heal the wounds that have kept you bound.

Kathy, one of our Mercy girls, had to learn to let herself cry and feel the pain from past events. After she acknowledged her pain, God was able to heal it. She also had to learn to express her feelings in ways that weren't hurtful to her or anyone else. That expression came through journaling, poetry, singing, and art. She also clung tightly to a few key scriptures. Even when her feelings told her differently, she hung on to the truth. One of the passages that served as a lifeline for her was Isaiah 53:3–4: "He was despised and rejected of men, a man of sorrows and acquainted with grief. And we hid, as it were, our faces from him; he was despised, and we did not esteem him. Surely he has borne our grief and carried our sorrows."

Jenny, a Mercy girl, did not let herself cry for years but found that crying is a great way to express emotions and release grief and pain of the past. She has had to learn the "skill" of crying. It still feels unnatural to her at times because she suppressed her feelings for so long, but she is getting a lot better at letting herself cry and feeling that release.

You too are allowed to cry and experience the wide range of emotions. There can be great release in tears. It is normal to feel hurt and angry and cheated and all of these things. Jesus Himself wept publicly, which tells us it can be emotionally healthy to do so. Your emotions help you to acknowledge the truth of what you went through—someone or something hurt you—and allow Jesus to heal your heart. By holding on to your pain you are denying Him the opportunity to comfort you and take that heavy burden from you. Jesus says, "Come to me, all you who are weary and burdened, and I will give you rest" (Matt. 11:28, NIV). If you don't take the step to come to Him, He can't give you rest.

Some people bury their hurts deep in a futile attempt to keep those wounds from affecting present-day life. But hurts just can't be forgotten. Shakespeare famously wrote that "the truth will out." That's true of hurts too. One way or another they will express themselves. Let me ask you, are you easily frustrated or angered around certain people or in certain situations? Are you sensitive to words and easily bruised by people's opinions? Are there subjects you just won't think about, places you won't go, people you won't see because the memory is too strong? Is there a need to control what happens around you so you don't get hurt again?

Healing from hurts means going back to where things started, like Cissy did with her rafting accident. What are your hurts? Who hurt you? What was the circumstance? Are you willing to relive those situations and invite God into the memories? Are you willing to let Him show you the truth of those situations from His perspective, and how He was guiding you through to the other side?

One of the counselors here at Mercy has a regular habit that I think is very healthy. When she feels herself getting uptight, irritable, and easily offended she takes some time to sit down and pray through her hurts. It often starts with a question: "God, I've been feeling uptight and angry about things. Why is that?" Sitting quietly she often hears the still, small voice pointing out things in her life that are bothering her. She writes them down on a piece of paper, says them aloud, and then forgives people and asks forgiveness of God for her own attitude. She then tears up the paper as a symbol of forgetting those hurts and spends time in worship to let God minister to her. That is a simple way you can address your own hurts—and not just the old, deep ones but the fresh, new ones you get in everyday life.

Some people write a letter breaking up with their former hurts and habits. "I'm done with you," the letters say. "I'm ending this relationship." That's an effective approach when the hurts and issues have become so personal that they are like a relationship.

You can also gird yourself for potentially hurtful situations. When our Mercy girls go home for holidays with family we get them good and prepared; otherwise they dance right into a bad, old dynamic. We have the girls cover their visits with prayer in advance. We have them list family members and choose to forgive them even before they have done anything wrong. We have them listen and let God speak about specific challenges that might come up. We encourage them to listen to podcasts and teachings on the drive home to give them tools and encouragement to handle difficult situations. When they walk into a bad atmosphere and their relatives are in a foul mood or stirring up strife, the girls don't take the bait. We teach them to say, "That's their stuff. I don't need to participate in anyone's bad attitude." We shore up their internal dialogue so they don't lose their freedom.

Moving Forward

Healing past hurts is a critical part of maintaining freedom even in bumpy circumstances. Ask yourself what your life would look like if you were completely healed of every hurt you still feel. What would you be doing differently? What would your attitude about the future be like? Would you be a more hopeful, optimistic person? Would you attempt more and do more? Would you treat people better?

The Bible gives great promises that we can move past our hurts:

> Do not remember the former things nor consider the things of old. See, I will do a new thing, now it shall spring forth; shall you not be aware of it? I will even make a way in the wilderness, and rivers in the desert.
>
> —ISAIAH 43:18–19

> Brothers, I do not count myself to have attained, but this one thing I do, forgetting those things which are behind and reaching forward to those things which are ahead, I press toward the goal to the prize of the high calling of God in Christ Jesus.
>
> —PHILIPPIANS 3:13–14

> Therefore, if anyone is in Christ, he is a new creation; old things have passed away; behold, all things have become new.
>
> —2 CORINTHIANS 5:17, NKJV

> Let us also lay aside every weight and the sin that so easily entangles us, and let us run with endurance the race that is set before us. Let us look to Jesus, the author and finisher of our faith.
>
> —HEBREWS 12:1–2

You may have been living in emotional survival mode for years, feeling that you have to take care of yourself and deal with your own pain without trusting anyone along the way. Friend, God not only listens to your heart and heals your wounds, but He will teach you how to live free of pain again. He is trustworthy. He will relieve you of your burdens as you lay them down at the feet of Jesus. Hold tightly to the Bible's promises:

The LORD is my pillar, and my fortress, and my deliverer; my God, my rock, in whom I take refuge; my shield, and the horn of my salvation, my high tower.
—PSALM 18:2

Now may the God of peace make you holy in every way, and may your whole spirit and soul and body be kept blameless until our Lord Jesus Christ comes again.
—1 THESSALONIANS 5:23, NLT

Don't spend one more day letting your past hurts guide you. By yourself or with the help of a good Christian counselor, face those hurts, see God in your past, and then move ahead with confidence.

Chapter 3

KEY #3: GETTING GOD'S PERSPECTIVE ON YOUR LIFE

I N 2012 KATE experienced a complete emotional shock when she found herself facing divorce. She and her husband had three girls, ages fourteen, twelve, and ten, and had been married more than twenty years. They attended church regularly as a family, and Kate had no real indication her husband was unhappy except for some ongoing financial and work-related struggles. It seemed he just suddenly wanted out.

Kate has worked for Mercy for many years. She came to us in 2006 and for six years had been immersed in the principles we teach at Mercy about forgiving others and walking in freedom no matter what life throws at us. Scriptural truth had become such a normal part of her thinking that when confronted with this life-changing situation she simply walked it out in real time.

Yes, the pain and confusion were still there, but Kate put those biblical tools to use—and found they worked. She was able to choose to forgive very early on and rest in her foundational relationship with Jesus. She kept renewing her mind and meditating on the Word. She listened to a lot of teaching podcasts and CDs on subjects she was dealing with. She allowed God to meet her in her everyday moments at her desk and at home with her kids. She listened to worship music almost constantly and found that God spoke to her through particular songs on many occasions. She would put headphones on at work and tell herself, "OK, from the beginning of work to lunch, I can make it." She even prayed while walking her dog.

By being in the Word so much she easily recognized the lies about her situation that might have tempted her to detour into bitterness, recrimination, and revenge. She also worked hard to avoid lies. She told me she could have listened to songs that say things like, "My husband left me, let's go have a beer," but that wouldn't have helped her make it through. In the immediate aftermath of what happened she chose to seek input from friends who were walking closely with God who could pray for her and encourage her from that perspective rather than friends and family she knew would rally to her defense in love but from a place of anger and protection. As a child of divorce herself, Kate wanted to walk it out well for her children and not go down the path of revenge and hostility. She remembered, "There is a way that appears to be right, but in the end it leads to death" (Prov. 14:12, NIV). It would have been easy to justify railing at her husband or spreading damaging information about him, but that wasn't how God told her to walk through it.

Kate was sitting at her desk one day when the phrase "Love God, love others" came to mind. She wrote it on a sticky note and put it on her desk. There it stayed for more than a year, a constant reminder of the path she was walking. She knew she was supposed to forgive and bless her ex-husband through the process regardless of what anyone thought she should do. Whenever she got riled up, she chose to forgive. Sometimes it was moment-by-moment. But she released it so she didn't have to carry the ugliness and bitterness.

Her friends who are not believers couldn't believe she was walking in such peace. They didn't understand how she could be OK in those circumstances.

"I've learned to say, 'I am a little kooky,'" Kate says. "But I've had a lot of opportunities to talk with people who say, 'How are you going through this with such peace? Are you really doing OK? Or are you faking it?' I was able to say, 'I am really doing OK, not because I'm such a great person. At times I wanted to go punch him. But by choosing to allow God into the brokenness and hurt, He helped me to respond in a way that was not my own. That comes from being exposed to the Word as much as I have been.'"

Kate took control of her thoughts when life went sideways. Instead of walking in terrible anger, bitterness, and depression, she put roots down deep and found rivers of peace.

HIGHER THOUGHTS

The Word of God says that when we renew our minds, our lives will be changed: "Don't copy the behavior and customs of this world, but let God transform you into a new person by changing the way you think. Then you will learn to know God's will for you, which is good and pleasing and perfect" (Rom. 12:2, NLT). Renewing your mind means to do away with ungodly thought patterns and to replace them with godly ones. It is impossible to do this without God's help. The world can help you change a behavior, but God helps you change your beliefs and actions, which begins with a change inside the human heart.

Some people think it's God's job to renew our minds and that our job is to sit passively by and let it happen without exerting any effort. But when we meditate on the Word and choose what we think, we are empowered to take a much more active role in changing our perspective. God never promised that no weapon will be formed against us but that no weapon formed against us will prosper (Isa. 54:17). When we latch on to His perspective on life, the weapons—the lies, fears, and hurts—will not prosper. We learn to actively break agreement with the enemy and tell him he is a liar. Renewing the mind doesn't mean waiting around for God to wash us clean. Instead we participate with Him to work out our own salvation in a practical way (Phil. 2:12).

Behind every bad habit or bondage is a lie. People speak lies to themselves every day.

- ❀ "It's not that big of a deal. It helps me get through the day."

- ❀ "I have to promote myself. Nobody else will do it for me."

- ❀ "Depression is just part of who I am. I'm a melancholy personality."

- ❀ "With the way I look, nobody could love me."

- ❀ "Given what happened to me in the past, I'm damaged goods."

- ❀ "God expects me to take care of myself. He only steps in when something is too big for me to handle."

And on and on. We play untrue thoughts through our heads so frequently that we essentially memorize them and convince ourselves that they are true. We write the scripts of our own lives based on lies supplied by the devil himself. Science tells us that repetitive thoughts over time become physical ruts in the brain that affect our reasoning, choices, and eventually our beliefs. Satan knows that once we are convinced that our thoughts are true, we will defend them even if they are ungodly. That's why he comes early in our lives to try to get us off the path of freedom.

Many people get saved at some point in life, but a smaller percentage learn to effectively renew their minds to what God is thinking. Some are not taught how to think God's thoughts. Others don't want to embrace the total commitment we talked about. They want God to save their souls but keep His hands off their minds and lifestyle. But total commitment must extend to every thought we have. We're not just climbing a fire escape to heaven. We commit our minds completely to Christ so that lies can be erased and He can do a powerful work of grace in us.

Imagine buying a new car and realizing it's missing the engine. That wouldn't be very useful. The Bible says that we were bought with a price by Jesus Himself (1 Cor. 6:20). He didn't buy part of us but all of us. We are owned by Him—every part of us. The Bible never tells us we can come to Jesus and keep control of our thought lives. Rather, it promises freedom through renewal of the mind. Romans 8:6 says that "to set the mind on the Spirit is life and peace" (ESV).

Some people freak out at the idea of committing their minds to Christ. They think it's like being part of some sort of cult or allowing their minds to be controlled. They ignore the fact that there are essentially only two choices in life: minds under the control of darkness or minds controlled by God's Spirit. Some people prefer the darkness they know to the light they don't know. Their lives reflect their choice: "If the light that is in you is darkness, how great is that darkness!" (Matt. 6:23). Notice that Jesus didn't say there was a third way. There is only light and darkness, and none of us can provide our own light.

Everything about our lives starts in the thought life. Thoughts become words; words become actions; actions create the life you are currently living. The enemy is focused intensely on your thought life because from it your whole life proceeds (Prov. 4:23). As with Adam and Eve in the garden, the enemy tries to blind us to our true identity and purpose. So many people live apart from their identity and purpose because they choose to believe lies. It doesn't make them bad people; it just means they are deceived. I'm raising my hand high on this one because I lived in deception for years before I was saved, and there are still areas where my thinking is wrong. My mind is being renewed all the time by God's Word and His Spirit. Getting God's perspective is a process, and if you don't keep moving forward you will fall into fresh new lies the enemy has for you.

God says in Isaiah 55:8:

> For My thoughts are not your thoughts, nor are your ways My ways, says the LORD.

Jesus says in John 8:31–32:

> If you abide in My word, you are My disciples indeed. And you shall know the truth, and the truth shall make you free.
>
> —NKJV

Romans 12:2 says:

> Do not be conformed to this world, but be transformed by the renewing of your mind, that you may prove what is the good and acceptable and perfect will of God.

Psalm 119:9 and 11 says:

> How can a young person stay on the path of purity? By living according to your word…I have hidden your word in my heart that I might not sin against you.
>
> —NIV

James 1:21 says:

> Receive with meekness the implanted word, which is able to save your souls.
>
> —NKJV

Let's look at basic ways to apply God's Word to everyday life to walk in greater freedom with each day.

You Can Choose What You Think

Some people think that whatever pops into their heads is what they have to think about. That's a recipe for disaster. Thinking is a choice. Just as you exercise control over your body and how you behave, so God expects you to exercise control over your mind and what you think. You choose your thoughts the same way you choose to forgive or choose to say yes to Christ. It takes your will saying "yes" and then your actions supporting that choice. The Holy Spirit gives you divine encouragement and empowerment to think the thoughts you have chosen to think—His thoughts, not ours. John says, "But if we walk in the light as He is in the light, we have fellowship one with another, and the blood of Jesus Christ His Son cleanses us from all sin" (1 John 1:7).

At this point your emotions will scream like a little child because they are used to controlling your mind. They used to set the agenda; they used to run the show. Paul said, "We all once lived in the passions of our flesh, carrying out the desires of the body and the mind, and were by nature children of wrath, like the rest of mankind" (Eph. 2:3, esv). People who live by their passions and feelings are by definition out of God's will. "For the mind that is set on the flesh is hostile to God, for it does not submit to God's law; indeed, it cannot" (Rom. 8:7, esv).

So here's what you do: Find the volume knob on your emotions and turn it way down. If your emotions don't agree with the Word of God then they are speaking lies to you. A commitment to Christ is not about how you feel. It is by faith. Inside of you is a faith muscle. The Bible calls it the measure of faith (Rom. 12:3). Just like any muscle it takes time and practice to isolate it, flex it, and feel it working. Soon you realize you're gaining strength. Your feelings and emotions will take notice. Everyone likes a winner, and after they see that faith muscle flexing and growing they will get on board. Your desires and attractions and opinions will actually change. This is why the Bible says so clearly for us to take an active role in choosing our thoughts:

> Set your mind on things above, not on things on the earth.
> —Colossians 3:2, nkjv

> Therefore lay aside all filthiness and remaining wickedness and receive with meekness the engrafted word, which is able to save your souls. Be doers of the word and not hearers only, deceiving yourselves. For if anyone is a hearer of the word and not a doer, he is like a man viewing his natural face in a mirror.
> —James 1:21–23

> Casting down imaginations and every high thing that exalts itself against the knowledge of God, bringing every thought into captivity to the obedience of Christ.
> —2 Corinthians 10:5

> Put off the former way of life in the old nature, which is corrupt according to the deceitful lusts, and be renewed in the spirit of your mind; and that you put on the new nature, which was created according to God in righteousness and true holiness.
> —Ephesians 4:22–24

None of the above scriptures mention accommodating your feelings or going wherever your emotions take you. It's impossible to accommodate your feelings and walk in freedom. It's like making a peace treaty with the devil and hoping to come out of it alive. Remember that the enemy has been empowering your negative, lying emotions to try to take your mind captive again.

He wants to cancel the power of that commitment you made to Christ. When he sees you're serious about kicking him out and choosing your thoughts rather than entertaining everything that comes into your head, he will probably try to make a deal with you for partial control.

The demonized people in Jesus's day always did this when Jesus came around. They shouted, "You are the Christ, the Son of God!" (Luke 4:41). One team of demons even begged Jesus to let them go into a herd of pigs rather than leave the area (see Mark 5). It seems possible that the demons hoped He would leave them alone if they declared who He was. But there's no such thing as a peace treaty with the devil. He's just postponing the battle until a later time. You can't say, "My household serves the Lord" while you're renting a room to the devil in your thought life. He'll never stay put. He'll start by raiding the fridge and running up your bills, then create division in your house, giving away your stuff and creating an atmosphere of suspicion and hatred, violence, and lust. There is no way to rent him a room without eventually giving him the whole house. He's not content just to be a boarder. He'll invite all his friends over, just like the Bible says (Matt. 12:44–45).

When people try to use their freedom in Christ to fulfill their own desires, it ends in disaster. The Bible warns:

> Live as people who are free, not using your freedom as a cover-up for evil, but living as servants of God.
> —1 PETER 2:16, ESV

> "All things are lawful to me," but not all things are helpful. "All things are lawful for me," but I will not be brought under the power of anything.
> —1 CORINTHIANS 6:12

For you were called to freedom, brothers. Only do not use your freedom as an opportunity for the flesh, but through love serve one another.
—Galatians 5:13, esv

Getting God's perspective means serving an eviction notice to the enemy and making a firm commitment to choose what we think. Then we begin to renovate our minds in specific, practical ways.

Meditating on the Truth

Valorie's dad was a chaplain in the military, so her family moved all the time. Valorie had difficulty adjusting to new settings and making new friends. She was also heavyset, which made it easy for other kids to tease her. They would call her fat and ugly, and say things like, "Valorie needs to watch her calories!" Over time, she thought that if so many different people said all of the same things, their words must be true. No boy had ever taken an interest in her so she believed she was unworthy of love and concluded that no man would ever marry her. Worse than that, she believed that not even God cared about her.

Those thoughts led Valorie down a road toward abusing her anxiety medication and getting into marijuana use. When she came to Mercy she, like all our residents, spent time each morning reading a passage of Scripture and discussing it with a staff member. During that time she developed a passion for the Word of God and a desire to understand it deeply. After she graduated, she started setting aside special time every day to read a section of the Bible and journal about it. Now she looks forward to this special time with the Lord every day and to what He has to say to her through His Word. She is walking in total freedom.

Valorie chose her thoughts and chose to meditate on God's Word. That choice brought amazing life and peace, just as the Bible promises.

> For God has not given us a spirit of fear, but of power and of love and of a sound mind.
> —2 TIMOTHY 1:7, NKJV

> This Book of the Law must not depart from your mouth. Meditate on it day and night so that you may act carefully according to all that is written in it. For then you will make your way successful, and you will be wise.
> —JOSHUA 1:8

> So then faith comes by hearing, and hearing by the word of God.
> —ROMANS 10:17

> Then Jesus said to those Jews who believed Him, "If you remain in My word, then you are truly My disciples. You shall know the truth, and the truth shall set you free."
> —JOHN 8:31–32

> Blessed is the man who walks not in the counsel of the ungodly, nor stands in the path of sinners, nor sits in the seat of scoffers; but his delight is in the law of the LORD, and in His law he meditates day and night. He will be like a tree planted by the rivers of water, that brings forth its fruit in its season; its leaf will not wither, and whatever he does will prosper.
> —PSALM 1:1–3

How many Christians do you know who are saved and go to church but who "walk in the counsel of the ungodly" in their social lives or the entertainment they consume or the kinds of conversations they have at work? To walk in freedom we must walk in the counsel of the godly in all areas of life. If you do that, you will make your own way prosperous and you will have good success. Light dispels the darkness. As the light of God's Word goes into your mind, it pushes the darkness out. Then the freedom of Christ begins to connect to your heart in a deeper way.

Here are some other passages to deeply consider:

Guide me in your truth and teach me, for you are God my Savior, and my hope is in you all day long.
—Psalm 25:5, NIV

Your word is a lamp to my feet and a light to my path.
—Psalm 119:105

Trust in the Lord with all your heart, and lean not on your own understanding; in all your ways acknowledge Him, and He will direct your paths.
—Proverbs 3:5–6

The steps of a good man are ordered by the Lord, and He delights in his way.
—Psalm 37:23, NKJV

Do you trust God to direct your paths? Do you meditate day and night on His Word? I have met a lot of people who grew up under legalistic systems and had people beat them up with the Word of God. Just because someone abused God's Word does not mean God's Word is bad. Almost anything on this earth can be used for good or evil. The devil even uses Scripture for his purposes. The first time he tempted Jesus in the desert, he didn't use Scripture. But when he saw that Jesus was basing his response on the Word, the devil changed tactics (see Matthew 4). He began twisting the Word to try to make it say what he wanted it to mean.

If we don't meditate on God's Word with the Holy Spirit guiding our understanding, we will be susceptible to the devil's twisted presentation of Scripture. If you have only a surface knowledge of the Bible, it's like taking a pocket knife to a modern battlefield. Get real—Paul said "the *weapons* of our warfare are not carnal" (2 Cor. 10:4, emphasis added). The weapon is in your mind and your mouth. It's called the Word of almighty God.

By rightly handling the Word of Truth we experience freedom, healing, and restoration. Even when God uses His Word to bring correction, He does it in such a way that it doesn't tear down or wound but builds up and heals. The key is to immerse ourselves in the Word. It says, "Faith comes by hearing, and hearing by the word of God" (Rom. 10:17). We need to hear it over and over again to remind ourselves of who we are in Christ. We need to speak it to ourselves with our mouths so our own ears hear our voice saying the truth. We need to stir ourselves up to remember. Peter said it was good for him to write the same things and remind you (2 Pet. 1:12–13).

You probably wouldn't even think about missing a meal, and yet God's Word is much more essential to our lives than food. Jesus quoted the Word when He said, "Man shall not live by bread alone, but by every word that proceeds out of the mouth of God" (Matt. 4:4). If we simply put as much dedication into eating the bread of life as we do physical food, our problems would surely be few. It is "life to those who find them, and health to all their body" (Prov. 4:22).

Living in freedom and getting God's perspective means hiding God's Word in your heart with regular, passionate meditation and memorization.

Replace Lies with the Truth

As the Word becomes the biggest part of our thought life and dialogue we can begin to go after those binding thoughts and false beliefs that keep us enslaved. Margaret grew up in a large, happy family and attended Catholic schools. She was quiet and mostly tried to go with the flow and stay out of the way at school.

One day in junior high Margaret's class was walking down the hall single file, and Margaret was minding her own business, when the principal nun singled her out, pushed her up against a wall, got nose-to-nose with her, and laid into her verbally. Margaret was so shocked by the unexpected confrontation that she didn't know how to respond.

"What did I do?" she asked, almost breathless.

"You know what you did," the nun replied, and stormed away.

Stunned and bruised emotionally, Margaret told herself the nun must have mixed her up with someone else. She didn't think about the incident much after that day, but something had changed inside of her that would affect her life much later.

Margaret had a similar experience when she went to high school. Many of the nuns at Margaret's school were precious and loving, but again the principal nun seemed angry and bent on punishing Margaret's entire class. She targeted certain leaders within the class, and to make sure she didn't draw their ire, Margaret laid low and was very compliant. She not only walked in great fear of the nun who had pushed her against the wall that day but also with those who seemed to use their position of authority in an intimidating manner.

Those memories faded away as Margaret raised her own family and journeyed through life. Twenty years after leaving high school Margaret came to work as a receptionist at Mercy and for some reason found herself bound up in fear. Her previous confidence evaporated, and she was terrified of failing the leaders in the ministry. Driven by this anxiety, she tried to do everything right and was meticulous about every little thing so she didn't "get into trouble." She noticed herself becoming overly compliant and people pleasing in a way she hadn't been before.

At Mercy the staff and directors go through the same curriculum as our residents in preparation for leading the girls. While going through that curriculum Margaret had a major moment of realization. For months she had wondered, "Why am I afraid of this and that person? Why am I so afraid to disappoint the women in spiritual leadership in this organization?" The Lord started speaking to her about how she viewed women in authority. While Margaret seldom thought about the incident with the nun, the Holy Spirit gently pointed out that since that time Margaret had not trusted women in spiritual leadership. The nuns and some of her own friends had made her feel so low and unworthy that Margaret had silenced her voice around women in spiritual leadership and felt an urgent need to never mess up around them. She didn't realize how much that fear of rejection impacted her.

Now the Lord made it clear that He was calling her back to her original purpose—spiritual leadership—but that first she had to be healed of past wounds. It wasn't an arduous process, she told me later. When she recognized that she needed to correct those thoughts and attitudes, she also felt the empowering of the Holy Spirit to help her. The key was that the revelation came from the Holy Spirit. He had chosen the time and place to do His work. In His infinite wisdom and care, God had placed Margaret in a ministry run almost entirely by women and put her around girls in our homes.

To get back on track, Margaret had to stop believing one set of things—"Women in spiritual leadership cannot be trusted. I must do everything perfectly to avoid their disapproval"—and start believing the truth—"Women and men in leadership can be trusted when they lead well, and my worth to them and to God is not based on doing everything perfectly." That process, very simply, is called getting God's perspective, or renewing our minds. It is at the very center of maintaining lifelong freedom in Christ.

Margaret now supervises the programs in each of our homes and recently became an ordained minister. The difference today, she says, is that she knows she is not going to get things right every time and no longer operates out of fear of making mistakes. Her natural confidence has returned and she feels free to share her ideas—and to provide gentle, encouraging leadership to other women.

At Mercy homes we work with the girls to make a list of lies they have believed. They are often things like:

❀"All men are bad. I can't trust any man."

❀"I'll never make a good wife."

❀"I'm ugly."

❀"If I were lovable nobody would have hurt me this way."

You remember Rachel, the woman who found freedom after sexual abuse by older men, abuse that had started at a young age. Rachel realized that the enemy had tried to silence her voice when she was young with a lie that went, "See? You tell someone about the abuse you suffer and it doesn't go anywhere." She found freedom the same way every believer should, by writing out scriptures and "truth statements" on cards and reading them silently and aloud. "I needed to hear myself speak the truth to counter the lies that were inside me," Rachel told me. "I got those lies out."

For example, when feeling anxious she would read the card that said, "I have the mind of Christ and He gives me peace." It pushed out the lie of anxiety and enabled her to step into the peace Jesus makes available.

Many people believe the lie that God abandoned them when they needed Him the most. But the truth is that "God is our refuge and strength, an ever-present help in trouble" (Ps. 46:1, NIV). We can say with confidence, "I will fear no evil; for You are with me; Your rod and Your staff, they comfort me" (Ps. 23:4).

We can hear God's voice to us in the words, "Do not fear, for I have redeemed you; I have called you by your name; you are Mine. When you pass through waters, I will be with you. And through the rivers, they shall not overflow you. When you walk through the fire, you shall not be burned, nor shall the flame kindle on you. For I am the LORD your God, the Holy One of Israel, your Savior" (Isa. 43:1–3).

Other people say, "I just have a hot temper. It's part of who I am—I can't do anything about it." They want to excuse their anger. The truth is that anger is a godly characteristic—but not crazy, blind, unforgiving anger, which is what people like to indulge in. Instead the Bible says, "Be angry but do not sin. Do not let the sun go down on your anger. Do not give place to the devil" (Eph. 4:26–27). If you are angry, be angry at principalities and powers, not at people. I admit that a hot temper is an area of weakness for me, but I don't excuse it. When I'm tempted to blow up, I pray scriptures like, "Lord, help me be quick to hear, slow to speak, slow to get angry," which is from James 1:19. "Help me to be angry but not to sin. Help me to be slow to anger, like You are, and for my anger to last for just a moment."

Still others have received a diagnosis or a label from a physician saying, "You are manic depressive" or, "You are bipolar" or, "You are schizophrenic." I'm here to tell you, you are not what you have been labeled. The Word of God labels you a son or daughter of the King of kings. The Bible labels you as free, because "if the Son sets you free, you shall be free indeed" (John 8:36).

Jesus got aggressive with the enemy, saying, "Get away from here, Satan! For it is written..." (Matt. 4:10). It's OK to yell at the devil sometimes. Put the nice you to the side and shout in his face. Maybe you need to do that figuratively or even literally with your problem, saying, "Away from me, Satan! For it is written..." Aggressively fight the schemes of the enemy. Fight as if your life depended on it, because it does. When he "roars" (1 Pet. 5:8), roar back!

The Word of God is our powerful weapon to defeat the enemy. When Jesus was tempted after fasting forty days, even He, the sinless, spotless Lamb of God, answered with, "It is written." If Jesus had to do that, how much more do we need to do it? Make "It is written" a regular part of your internal conversation and thought life. It works against all kinds of temptation and lies. Proverbs 3:5–6, a well-known verse, tells us to "Trust in the LORD with all your heart, and lean not on your own understanding." When we don't renew our minds, we naturally lean on our own understanding because that's all there is for us. But if you renew your mind to God's Word and His way, you will walk in more and more freedom day by day, moment by moment.

You might think, "But I did those things. These aren't lies; they're the truth." Did you know there is a difference between facts and truth? The devil can speak facts, but he cannot speak truth. The blood of Jesus covers all the facts of your sin, and the truth becomes that you are clean and spotless before God. See the difference?

Take a look at the apostle Paul's amazing example. Paul was involved in persecuting and killing believers in the early church. But later he wrote to the church at Corinth, "We have wronged no one, we have corrupted no one, and we have defrauded no one" (2 Cor. 7:2). You might read that and say Paul is lying because he admitted elsewhere that he wronged many people. But God removes our sins from us as far as the east is from the west when we confess our sin and repent. We are dead to sin and alive unto God (Rom. 6:11).

Paul could say he didn't wrong anyone because the old Paul was dead. He didn't identify with his past anymore. He said, "forgetting what lies behind and straining forward to what lies ahead, I press on toward the goal for the prize of the upward call of God in Christ Jesus" (Phil. 3:13–14, ESV). When your old man is dead and gone, you are a new creation. The truth about you is found not in the facts of your previous life but in what the Bible says about you.

Steps to Getting God's Perspective

I'm going to ask you to do what so many hundreds of Mercy girls do to get God's perspective on their lives. I want you to summarize, personalize, and vocalize the Word of God. Here is an explanation of each step.

Summarize it

As you meditate on Scripture and hear teachings or read devotionals, listen for God's voice as He speaks into your life through those resources. When a certain verse or passage of the Bible hits your ear and becomes life to you, summarize it in your own words. This will cause you to draw out the meaning in a fuller way, considering every aspect of it. By putting it in your own words you will process the meaning and "digest" it more completely.

Write that summary down in a journal, on an index card, or in the notes application in your smartphone—somewhere you can revisit it later.

Personalize it

Then ask God what He is saying to you personally through this scripture so that you can speak it aloud. The Holy Spirit speaks to us through the Word, illuminating certain truths specifically for us at just the right time. How many times have you read a verse that you have read many times before only to find that this time it jumps off the page and virtually glows with life and meaning? That is the Holy Spirit personalizing the scripture to your immediate circumstance. Pay attention to those moments and meditate on those verses of Scripture. Give Him time to talk to you about how they relate to your situation.

Ask God, what does this scripture mean for me now? How can I put it to work in my life?

Vocalize it

Finally, vocalize that scripture and your summary by reading them out loud. Don't be content to think it in your head. There is a place for silent contemplation and reading, but this is not that time. I want you to move your lips and let your own ears hear your voice. Read the scripture aloud and then read your summary aloud. It may feel embarrassing at first but over time it will powerfully align your heart and your mind with what God is telling you in and through His Word. Go ahead—read it out loud!

Here's a walk-through example:

> The thief comes only to steal and kill and destroy; I have come that they may have life, and have it to the full.
> —John 10:10, niv

1. *Summarize*: The devil is a thief who wants to take everything from me, decimate my life, and murder me, if he can. Jesus came so that I can live and have

everything I need, including life at its fullest and most satisfying.

2. *Personalize*: God, I know the devil wants to take from me, put an end to my life, and render my work ineffective, but thank You that You came to give me life, and not just life but life at its very best! Please show me how to have that life, and how to resist the thief in areas where he is working to destroy me.

3. *Vocalize*: (Say it all out loud!)

I want to encourage you to take the truths from God's Word that you are discovering and vocalize them on a daily basis. Every morning during daily Bible reading at the Mercy homes, the residents and staff confess scriptures aloud. Just as God spoke the world into existence, when you speak His Word out loud, it has power beyond anything we can see. Speaking Scripture aloud plants it inside of you and brings life. As Proverbs 18:21 says, "Death and life are in the power of the tongue, and those who love it will eat its fruit."

If you don't know where to start, try reading all of Psalm 119, the longest chapter in the Bible. I find it to be an awesome and virtually inexhaustible handbook for renewing the mind. Take it bit by bit, pausing whenever you want to summarize, personalize, and vocalize it.

I used this very practical strategy against the lies in my own head when I was first born again. I was living under a sense of guilt and condemnation because I was sin-conscious rather than righteousness-conscious. Being sin-conscious means being hung up all the time with what you've done wrong and how you'll never measure up in your own strength. Then somebody shared with me books about faith, the power of confessing God's Word, our authority as believers, and knowing who we are in Christ. I began to study the idea of being righteousness-conscious instead of sin-conscious, and I'll never forget when it hit my heart as a reality that I am accepted in the beloved, not because I had a perfect day but because righteousness is a state that we can live in. We are the righteousness of God in Jesus Christ and all our sin—past, present, and future—is forgiven. That's not a license to sin. It's freedom to live right. I read aloud Psalm 103:10, which says, "He does not treat us as our sins deserve or repay us according to our iniquities" (NIV). I read, "For God did not send His Son into the world to condemn the world, but that the world through Him might be saved" (John 3:17).

By speaking the Word and putting it in my own words I tore down those wrong ways of thinking. I continue to do the same thing today. You never outgrow the Word of God. It is a seed that goes into you and produces fruit. If the Holy Spirit alerts me that I need to walk in more love, I read 1 Corinthians 13:4, "Love is patient, love is kind" (NIV). That means God's love is in me, and I am supposed to be patient and kind. The seed of that truth goes into me and produces patience and kindness. The Word is called the "perfect law of liberty" (James 1:25) and the apostle James said that by looking into it we find true freedom and life. Looking into it, speaking it aloud, meditating on it—it's all part of the process of internalizing and growing the truth in our own hearts and minds.

Lastly, let me urge you to obey God's voice. As your perspective comes in line with His, undoubtedly He will begin to tell you things to do and changes to make. These are often very practical: "Go back to school and get your degree." "Join this or that Bible study." "Stop by that friend's house. She needs comfort." "Sign up your daughter for ballet lessons." Obey those promptings! You never know where they will lead. He orders our steps *in His Word* (Ps. 119:133). He doesn't order our entire life for us to see. He doesn't even show us our entire week or our entire day. Rather,

He orders our steps. If He's leading you to do something or make some change, don't wait for the money or time or convenience—just do it. Chances are you won't get any more direction until you take the step He told you to take.

Getting God's perspective is a lifelong process. It will change who you are. If you take these steps, in one year you will hardly recognize yourself. That transformation will continue and you will wonder how you came so far so fast. That is the power of agreeing with God—it brings life, peace, and countless good things. And you will have less baggage and a greater sense of freedom with each day.

Chapter 4

KEY #4: CHOOSING TO FORGIVE

A S A COLLEGE-AGED woman, Rachel moved away from home to attend seminary and work at a Christian organization. There she became good friends with an older family who took her in and treated her as one of their own. The husband worked at the Christian organization and the wife worked at the nearby Christian college. But when the wife died, Rachel and the husband began to grieve the loss together. Though he was nearly forty years older than Rachel, the man initiated an emotional and sexual relationship with Rachel that they both knew was wrong.

Fearing that he would lose his position, reputation, and income, the man begged Rachel not to reveal their secret to anyone. Over the course of three years their relationship became increasingly enmeshed. They worked in the same building with the same people, ran in the same social circles, and even had the same car insurance agent. The man wanted Rachel to report to him whom she had talked with every day because he dreaded the relationship being exposed.

They successfully hid their relationship, but Rachel began to experience what she describes as a gradual but severe breakdown. She had been sexually abused as a child, and the pain of those memories returned with a vengeance and compounded her confusion. Though she lived, worked, and studied in a completely Christian environment, she became so depressed that she was hospitalized three times and for the first time in her life became suicidal. Her coworkers were perplexed but strangely passive. No one came alongside her to offer help. Rachel used up all her sick time, vacation time, and unpaid time just to stay home.

Seeing no other way out, and concerned that she would one day kill herself just to end the relationship, she quit her job and withdrew from seminary, though she loved being a student. During a stay at the hospital she decided to confess to a hospital psychiatrist about the inappropriate relationship she was having. Instead of helping her, the psychiatrist himself initiated an inappropriate relationship with her. When Rachel protested that it was unethical and wrong he promised her, "The guidelines between doctor and patient are outdated."

Within a week of being discharged he raped her and then invited her to stay at his house because she had lost her apartment.

"At that point I could see the evil growing darker. I was trapped," Rachel says. "I didn't want anything to do with ministry, with God, with the church. I didn't feel like I could even go back to the hospital because it was no longer a safe place."

She fled to her parents' home sixteen hours away and slept for what felt like days. With the help of good Christian counseling she began wanting to live again. The Lord did a deep work in her heart. Still, she kept asking God, "How did I let myself fall into this? Why wasn't I smart enough to avoid it? Why didn't I see it coming?" God began showing her that she had spoken up to defend herself, but men who should have protected her had used her instead.

God took Rachel on a journey of forgiveness. Soon she was able to pray for the man at the Christian organization who had drawn her into an affair. She hoped the Lord would bless his life and allow him to remarry. She never spoke to him again, but she genuinely wanted good things for him.

She also felt obligated to tell the organization about what had happened, and was surprised when they said they did not believe her because this man and his character were supposedly so impeccable. She provided bank statements totaling tens of thousands of dollars he had paid her to stay silent, and phone records showing they had spent hours a day on the phone. He soon confessed his inappropriate relationship to his employer and went through a disciplinary process.

Rachel also filed a complaint with the hospital about the psychiatrist, who has since moved on to a series of jobs at hospitals in other cities. An investigation is under way that may spare other young women the same injustice Rachel experienced. Even then, Rachel came to a place of such confidence in Christ that she could pray for his soul and want him to come to salvation, though she didn't want him to have access to vulnerable girls.

Most meaningful of all to her, Rachel returned to seminary and earned her master of arts degree in counseling. Not long after that she was hired at Mercy.

"My life has become more than I ever imagined," she told me. "Psalm 18 says, 'He has put my feet in spacious places.' God has done that for me. My mind and heart are free. I can walk wherever I want to go. My story is about what the Lord has done in my life through the pain. I learned about His character, that He is good."

Rachel's amazing story of forgiveness is a story of finding freedom. That same freedom is available to you.

FORGIVING GOD

One of the biggest hang-ups people have as they get rid of their personal baggage and walk in freedom is their offense toward God. Deep down many people believe God has treated them or someone else unfairly and so they elect to ignore Him. They are in effect "punishing" God for His "wrongs," giving Him the silent treatment, deliberately remaining distant and angry. After all, how can you love someone who has the power to stop evil but still allows child molestation, disease, and a thousand other horrible things—not to mention the ugly things that happen to us personally?

This mentality may describe you at some level. Are you holding God responsible for some injustice you suffered? Or for pain in the world around you? It's useful to take a moment and consider, is God on the hook with you? How do you perceive Him—as being all good or just mostly good? Totally trustworthy or just mostly so? Being honest with ourselves about these things makes a big difference in our level of freedom. Many Christians maintain a professional distance from God because they simply don't trust Him. They harbor anger against Him for pain they experienced and even think that God somehow ordained their pain.

At Mercy, we take girls through a simple exercise of visualizing how they see God. The idea is to shed light on their relationship with Him. Some picture Him sitting on a throne, and they see themselves close to Him. Others see themselves very far away from Him. Some see Him as a good father and some as a threatening authority figure. We had one girl who saw God as the Stay Puft Marshmallow Man from the 1980s movie *Ghostbusters*, stomping through a city and wrecking everything in His path, all while wearing a big, cheesy smile.

Maybe your visual is funny too—and illuminating.

How do you see God? What mental picture do you have for Him? When you picture yourself with Him, what is the context? Are you relating to each other or is He far away and concerned with other things? What is your emotional posture toward Him? Do you feel joy, pain, fear, peace? Your response may tell you a lot about the health of your relationship with Him and how close you really want to be to Him.

One of the basic deceptions and most effective traps of the enemy is to cause people to confuse the devil's work and God's will. You might have heard the verse in James 1:17 that says, "Every good gift and every perfect gift is from above and comes down from the Father of lights." That's a wonderful promise all on its own, but the verse right before it tells us something just as important: "*Do not be deceived.* Every good and perfect gift comes from God" (see James 1:16–17). James was emphasizing that the enemy deceives people into thinking God is the author of evil. It is one of the enemy's deadliest tools of all time.

When people believe that God hurt them, it drives a huge wedge between them and God. Can you imagine loving, trusting, and worshipping a God who planned and caused your deepest pain? When people who have been abused and trampled on hear that God has a plan for their lives they usually say, "If God's plan looks like what I've experienced, I don't want anything to do with Him."

Let's be really clear: There are two plans for your life. God has a plan for you, and the devil has a plan for you too. And they couldn't be more opposed to each other.

God's plan is to make you a literal dwelling place for God. This started the day you were born again. He began building you into a dwelling place so beautiful and full of love, peace, and power that it would blow your mind if you got a glimpse of the full reality. How cool is it that the God who spoke the universe into existence chooses to literally live in us though we are simple jars of clay? His plan is to make you awe-inspiring and glorious.

The devil's plan is quite different. Even the roach-infested home I described earlier would be cozy compared to his ultimate plan for you. The devil wants you to suffer forever in separation from God, undergoing hideous forms of torture and pain without end. He wants to separate you from God now and confuse you so you don't see and feel God's goodness. He cannot force you to shut the door on God because of your free will to choose; but He can make a strong case for you to shut the door by appealing to your pain and human logic.

It's almost inconceivable but true that you have been given the power to choose which plan you want to follow. You can choose life and God's plan, or you can choose death and the devil's plan. This power to choose is the greatest, most far-reaching power we have as human beings. We may do many great things—rule nations, create brilliant inventions or works of art, and rise to the highest levels of fame and fortune. But the choice to say yes or no to God remains our most awesome power. With it we literally choose our eternal destiny by choosing our relationship with God.

You have that power right now. With it you choose how you are going to walk with Him today, tomorrow, and forever. If we blame Him in our hearts, maligning His character by holding on to unforgiveness, then we choose the devil's plan instead of God's and invite a measure of death into our situation.

Let's take this moment to shut the biggest door of deception in the entire universe. Say this aloud:

God is never bad.

The enemy is never good.

If you hold on to those two truths no matter what happens to you, it will save you years and even a lifetime of stumbling around in darkness and confusion thinking that God is the author of your pain. No! He is the author of your deliverance and joy. The enemy is the enemy, not God. We don't base this on our own opinions or on some fairy tale but on the sure Word of God, which says:

He who sins is of the devil, for the devil has sinned from the beginning. For this purpose the Son of God was manifested, that He might destroy the works of the devil.

—1 JOHN 3:8, NKJV

Jeremiah 29:11 tells us, "For I know the plans I have for you," declares the LORD, "plans to prosper you and not to harm you, plans to give you hope and a future" (NIV). In John 10:10 Jesus said, "The thief does not come, except to steal and kill and destroy. I came that they may have life, and that they may have it more abundantly."

Never in the Bible is anything good attributed to Satan, and the Bible tells us with absolute certainty that God is perfect in love. He has never done a wrong thing. He has only done good to you since the day you were conceived. That means it was never in God's will that you were hurt or rejected or scarred by another person. His love for you was so great that He sent Jesus to pay the penalty and take the pain away from you. His heart was broken so that yours could be healed.

Now He wants to give back to you everything that the enemy has stolen. Isaiah 61:7 says, "Instead of your shame you shall have double honor." At Mercy homes we constantly speak scriptures like these out loud to ourselves and to one another so that we are grounded in truth, not in some human opinion or manmade counseling theory. We're not in the business of rebuilding girls' lives on whatever advice is featured in the latest issue of Oprah's magazine. We are laying a sure foundation that cannot be shaken.

People so often get caught up in the "why." "Why did this happen to me? Why did God allow it?" The answer is simple: Someone did evil to you, or you chose evil for yourself. We live on a fallen planet. It happens all the time. Humanity lives in the valley of decision. God appeals to each one of us: choose life!

As long as you keep this fact in mind—that God is never bad and the devil is never good—you will always walk in light and understanding. You will not blame God for awful things. Rather, you will grieve with Him over the pain in this world, and you will work to bring His plan into action in places the enemy has tried to burn to the ground.

Unfortunately, some religious people help the devil by speaking a strange view of God's sovereignty. They say, "God is God and whatever happens is His will." This line of thinking may sound logical, but it completely ignores the fact that He has given us free will to choose good or evil. It makes God the author of good and evil, which is not biblical.

My sister's husband was a great guy, one of the kindest people I've ever met. He was killed by a drunk driver on his way home one night. Was it God's will for that driver to be drunk and to get behind the wheel? Of course not. The Bible says we must obey the laws of the land out of respect for God's established authorities. The drunk driver was not obeying the laws of the land. This was a manmade tragedy based on the human will and bad choice of a person who ended up taking an innocent life. He took the awesome power God has put in our hands and used it for bad. When people follow the enemy, he can work through them to hurt innocent people because they are in "the snare of the devil, after being captured by him to *do* his will" (2 Tim. 2:26, emphasis added).

God did not plan and cause that accident. But He has redeemed it in my sister's life. He can take any evil and use it for good. If you need proof, just look in the mirror. All of us have done evil to other people. Most people who are angry at God like to focus on the evil done to them but not on the evil they themselves have done. Friend, look at your own life. Did God make you lie to that person and hurt her feelings? Did God make you sin sexually or get drunk or steal? No, you chose to sin all on your own. The truth is, you've done wrong to people as well. You may have even hurt someone very badly. We're all capable of it. I have yet to meet someone who has not hurt someone badly at some point in life. All of us mess up. But we tend to downplay the wrong we have done and play up what others have done to us. We even blame God for our pain while overlooking our hurtful actions.

One young lady came to a Mercy home from the state of New York. She was sixteen years old, pregnant, and every time I saw her, she was crying. Finally, I stopped her in the hall and said, "Every time I see you, you're crying. Is there something I can help you with? Why are you so upset? I understand you're pregnant, but you're here, you're in a safe place, you have great food and people caring for you. What's going on?"

She replied bitterly, "I'm mad at God!"

I said, "Tell me why you're mad at God."

She said, "I don't understand why God let me get pregnant."

I saw this would take some time so I invited her into my office for a sit-down chat.

"Sweetheart," I said, "let me ask you a question. Do you see that highway out there? What if I went and laid down in the middle of that highway and got hit by a truck? An ambulance takes me to the hospital and you come to visit me. I'm all broken up and bruised. What if I said to you, 'Why did God let this happen to me?' What would you say to me?"

"That you shouldn't have laid down in the middle of the road."

"Girl, that's exactly what I'm saying to you. God did not let you get pregnant. You made a choice that produced a consequence. Getting pregnant is about the sperm and the egg hitting at the right time. You made that choice and the result is this child you're carrying. You're mad at the wrong person. You made the choice."

Maybe for the first time she realized that God wasn't just up there directing everything that happened. She saw the amazing power of choice and the need to take personal responsibility for her choice rather than blaming God for the outcome of what she had done.

"The truth is that God is not mad at you or ashamed of you. He is proud of you for choosing life," I said. "God provided a place like Mercy for you and your child to receive life and love. He is with you!"

That girl chose to quit being mad at God. Today that child of hers is a teenager, and she has the joy of raising him.

The good news of the gospel is that even in a world where so many people choose evil, we can choose to love and walk in freedom. Sin is in the earth. But so is love, and love is greater. David said in Psalm 23:4, "Even though I walk through the valley of the shadow of death, I will fear no evil." Each of us walks through that valley, but the promise of God is that we don't have to fear it and that He is with us! It does not need to control our emotions. Rather, Paul says our mind is controlled by the Spirit (Rom. 8:6), and that "Christ's love compels us" (see 2 Corinthians 5:14). We can walk in freedom no matter what. David continued, "You prepare a table before me in the presence of my enemies" (Ps. 23:5). Notice that God did not simply wipe out David's enemies but rather gave David a wonderful life right in their presence. He wants to do the same for you.

God has never done you wrong. In fact, He's done you such good that it will take eternity to understand and appreciate it all. He literally stepped between you and the worst evil you could ever experience—eternal separation from Him—and provided a way for you to enjoy His presence and peace now and forever. Isaiah 53 says, "Surely he took up our pain and bore our suffering" (v. 4, NIV). Friend, you are "accepted in the Beloved" (Eph. 1:6, NKJV).

Imagine that—a God who loves so vastly and immeasurably that He suffered much worse evil than you or I have ever suffered, all so He could relieve us of the burdens of guilt and shame and personal pain. God doesn't deserve our blame: He deserves our unending gratitude—and our very lives.

I hope this gives you a sense of the depth and power of forgiveness. It is not just about letting someone off the hook; it's about understanding what God's character is and then declaring it through a life lived in freedom and forgiveness toward others.

Forgiving the Jerk Who Hurt Us

Forgiving God is one thing. Forgiving other people—well, don't they deserve our blame?

Trish, who works here at Mercy, was saved at age eight and grew up in church with parents who loved the Lord. She married a Christian boy she had met in high school who came from a believing family as well. Trish just knew they had the same values and were moving in the same direction with God.

But the end of her marriage came suddenly. One day her husband told her he had never loved her and that he was leaving. Trish did not see it coming, and it shocked everyone in their circle of friends. To make it worse, their daughter was fifteen months old when he left.

Trish soon realized that she had placed a great deal of confidence in her husband and marriage instead of in the Lord. She had made her husband and family an idol, looking to him to fix everything in her life and to supply all her emotional and spiritual needs. She repented of those things, but her heart was filled with grief. She didn't trust anybody, and the foundation of her life seemed hopelessly broken. She had lived right, gone to church, attended premarital counseling, married a Christian, faithfully attended Bible studies, and planned to raise her kids in the church. Divorce was never on her radar. Pretty much every dream she had for her life lay shattered.

She found herself going before the Lord and asking questions like, "Are You even real? Everything I feel I was standing on is gone." There were many tears and conversations and much yelling at the Lord, but she persisted in this, and little by little God began to prove Himself. He revealed to her that He was real and trustworthy in her everyday life. He met her financial and emotional needs. He took care of her daughter's needs. But it took time.

The hardest thing for Trish was forgiving her ex-husband and not allowing bitterness to take root. Like a gardener determined to keep the soil free of weeds, she dug up bitterness wherever it sprouted. She realized that forgiveness does not come naturally—she had to learn to forgive. Listening to CDs about forgiveness gave her tools and challenged her to grow. She also found that learning to serve others took her mind off herself. Immersing her soul in praise and worship and listening to other people's testimonies reminded her how great and faithful God is, and how much He forgives us.

Trish looks back now and knows she was saved before, but her relationship with Christ was never as real as it is now. He gives her the power to raise her daughter as a single parent, and gives her the power to forgive her ex-husband.

"I know now Jesus is my all in all," she said to me recently. "The Lord can take any evil and turn it for good. He continually shows us how faithful He is, how true His Word is."

When someone hurts you, the enemy will appeal to your sense of reason and outrage. He wants you to believe that forgiveness doesn't make sense, that it's dangerous, idealistic, and unfair. Like flies drawn to a wound, the enemy comes to exploit your pain. But as Trish forgave her former husband, and Rachel forgave those who selfishly used her for their own gratification, we can close up the wounds by forgiving everyone—even our worst offenders.

When I was a new believer it wasn't even on my radar screen to forgive. I was happy about my relationship with God but there were still people I was mad at. Then one day I came across a scripture in Matthew 6:14–15 where Jesus said, "For if you forgive men for their sins, your heavenly Father will also forgive you. But if you do not forgive men for their sins, neither will your Father forgive your sins."

That sounded pretty ironclad to me. I didn't see wiggle room. I certainly wanted God's forgiveness, and to get it I had to forgive others. Psalm 119:89 says, "Forever, O LORD, Your word is established in heaven," and Psalm 89:34 says, "My covenant I will not violate nor alter the word that has gone out from My lips." I knew Jesus's command to forgive was not just a suggestion and that He wouldn't be making any exceptions for Nancy Alcorn. I had to learn how to forgive.

He won't make exceptions for any of us. To walk in freedom we must become experts at forgiving others—not just benchwarmers but power sluggers. We want to be so good at forgiving that we make the Forgivers All-Star Team. I promise you it's the only way to walk in total freedom and avoid falling into traps of bitterness.

I sometimes wonder what Jesus Himself had to forgive. He clearly had a strained relationship with His brothers, who on at least two occasions mocked Him and said He was crazy (Mark 3:21, John 7:5). I imagine that reflected their relationship growing up as well. You can see the tensions that lay under the surface in His earthly family.

Jesus also seemed to have lost the man who served as His earthly father. Joseph, Mary's husband, is not seen after Jesus was twelve. Anyone who has lost a parent before their time knows what a gap that leaves in your life. It seems possible to me that Jesus had to remind Himself that God is good and never evil during that difficult season of loss.

Then, of course, Jesus forgave His own murderers as He was dying, and His words give us a key to how He walked in freedom from bitterness: "Father, forgive them, for they do not know what they are doing" (Luke 23:34, NIV).

Have you ever done something so dumb that you look back and go, "How on earth did I decide to do that?" All of us act in ignorance sometimes. In our ignorance the devil can use us to do harm. One of the best ways to make forgiving easier is to always remind yourself that people are not our enemy—our enemy is the enemy. People often act in ignorance or plain, blind selfishness. The Bible tells us that the powers of darkness are motivating and working in people who are disobedient, "having been taken captive by him [Satan] to do his will" (2 Tim. 2:26, NKJV).

Paul wrote that "our fight is not against flesh and blood, but against principalities, against powers, against the rulers of the darkness of this world, and against spiritual forces of evil in the heavenly places" (Eph. 6:12). This is not some spooky, vague idea; it's a concrete truth. The people who hurt you were motivated and urged on by the enemy, often against their better judgment and often in blindness to the consequences. Those people did not mean to hurt you, and even if they did, "they did not know what they were doing."

Just as we shouldn't ascribe bad motives and evil things to God, we should keep in mind that when people do evil they are under the power of the evil one. Forgiveness, then, is not just about our emotional health, it's about spiritual warfare. To withhold forgiveness, according to the Scriptures:

❈ Is a form of wrestling with flesh and blood, which wastes time and wears you out physically and emotionally

❈ Takes your attention and strength off the real enemy of your soul

❈ Gives anger control over you: "And 'don't sin by letting anger control you.' Don't let the sun go down while you are still angry, for anger gives a foothold to the devil" (Eph. 4:26–27, NLT)

❈ Gives the devil room to bring death into your situation

❈ Keeps God from forgiving you, as Scripture says, "And when you stand praying, forgive if you have anything against anyone, so that your Father who is in heaven may also forgive you your sins" (Mark 11:25)

This is serious stuff. Forgiveness is literally the power to overcome what the devil meant for harm. He wants the ripple effect of hurt and abuse to go on for generations. You have heard the saying, "Hurt people hurt people." That is the devil's design. But God has put it within our grasp to stop the devil's plan by forgiving. Just as we are saved by faith and not feelings, so also we are empowered to forgive by faith and not feelings. We can forgive without even wanting to! In fact, that's exactly how it works—by choice.

Forgiving others is one of the most important ways we exercise our power to choose God. It's not too grandiose to say that when we forgive others, we rule the universe. We put the enemy under our feet and become more like the One who holds everything together by the power of His Word. We are told to be "imitators of God" (Eph. 5:1) and to prepare ourselves to rule and reign with Him one day (Rev. 20:4, 6). God offers forgiveness to everyone, even when they work against Him. You and I should do the same.

In this life we get plenty of opportunities to forgive. You and I can forgive others the same way God forgives us. How? By choice and by consistent practice. When someone hurts you, whether it's at paper cut level or massive personal trauma level, simply say, "I choose to forgive that person for what he or she did." Like a puppy on a leash, your feelings will be straining to go the other way. Your job is to teach them to heel and follow where you choose to go.

It's extremely important to ground yourself into the following scriptures and let them sink into the garden of your heart like drops of rain.

> Be kind one to another, tenderhearted, forgiving one another, just as God in Christ also forgave you.
> —EPHESIANS 4:32;
> see also vv. 29–31

> Make allowance for each other's faults, and forgive anyone who offends you. Remember, the Lord forgave you, so you must forgive others.
> —COLOSSIANS 3:13, NLT

> Bear with each other and forgive one another if any of you has a grievance against someone. Forgive as the Lord forgave you.
> —COLOSSIANS 3:13, NIV

Then spend time with God talking about what happened to you. You might write down your thoughts and feelings. David did that a lot, and the result is dozens of psalms in the Bible. The Book of Psalms is like a prayer journal of what David and others were experiencing and feeling. It wasn't all pretty. They were super honest with God about the good, bad, and ugly they were feeling. You can be too. God can carry the weight of it. He's very good at listening.

When girls come to our Mercy homes they know they have tried everything else and nothing has worked. Maybe you're at that place. Relationships are crashing down; finances, dreams, and hopes are gone. You know you need a better relationship with God to get through what you're going through. This is your time to hash it out. Get honest and have an emotionally candid conversation with God. I'm here to tell you, yelling can be a form of prayer. God is not afraid of volume. Your words and tone might frighten you but not Him. He knows those things are inside you already, and it's a lot better to get them out than to let them continue to fester. If you have a sincere desire to connect with God and are not just indulging your bitterness and making the problem worse, then airing your emotions to Him can move you toward a better relationship with Him.

I know a lot of people who try to win the battle of the mind without ever bringing the fight into the visible realm. It all takes place inside of them. The enemy keeps people in bondage for years with the fear of expressing what's inside. He lies and says that God will be offended by their words or can't handle their emotions. Believe me, if God were easy to offend, I would have done it by now. If you're mad at Him, say you're mad at Him. If you don't understand what's going on, say you don't understand what's going on.

Then get ready for His response—He will be honest right back with you. He will probably tell you whom you need to forgive and what you need to do to get back to the path of freedom. That's exactly what you want: an honest conversation, a frank assessment, a real plan. It's like opening the wound to clean it out. It can seem scary, but it's the only way to keep the infection of bitterness from defiling your soul.

We also counsel some girls to make a list of people and offenses and say, "I choose to forgive this person for this." That may be a helpful exercise for you. Be specific about it. Not just, "I forgive my husband for being a jerk," but, "I forgive my husband for forgetting Valentine's Day." Or, "I forgive my wife for neglecting me when she's busy." It's a way of acknowledging it to God in prayer and taking back power. Up to that point the offense had power over you. When you forgive you do what Jesus did and gain ultimate freedom. Some people later tear that list up or burn it. One time we actually put a girl's list through a shredder, which gave her a practical visual of total forgiveness.

If you have a tough time even thinking about forgiving someone, consider that there are people who are thinking the same thing about you. Though it may be difficult to imagine, you have been on the other side of an offense more times than you care to know. Try to recall a time when you hurt someone, whether on purpose or by accident. Did you want them to hold that offense against you? Couldn't you feel their grudge like a weight pressing against your own soul? Didn't you long for them to forgive you, not because you deserved it but because it was the only way out of the trap for both of you? Forgiveness opens the door to restoration and freedom—for you and the person you have chosen to forgive.

When we recognize that we have been forgiven much, then we love much (Luke 7:47). Living in love is what living in freedom is all about.

GOD IS YOUR PROTECTOR AND VINDICATOR

My friend Jane was good at gymnastics and dance in junior high school. She set high standards for herself and wanted to perform up to them. In everyday life Jane was shy and reserved, but once she walked onto the floor to do a beam routine or a dance routine, she had all the confidence in the world. It was almost like there was a performance button she could push. She believed the person she was on the floor was her "real" self.

In junior high she attended school with a girl who was a bit of a bully. Jane had the habit of walking with straight posture because of her dance and gymnastics training. She was also quiet, which gave some people the impression that she was stuck up. One day in the hallway this bully started making fun of Jane in front of other people. She said ugly things about Jane, claiming that she walked around with her nose in the air because she thought she was better than everyone else.

Though Jane normally avoided attention and confrontation, this time was different. She unleashed on the bully, getting right in the girl's face and letting her have it. Everyone was astonished at what normally quiet Jane was doing, but the girl had touched a nerve by criticizing something so close to Jane's heart. It was the only time Jane ever blew up like that in junior high school, and the story actually has a nice ending: Jane and this girl went on to become very good friends.

Jane stood up for herself, which can be good, but in a way she also was getting vengeance on a girl who had a reputation for mouthing off and putting people down. Many of us have gone through much more serious situations where the hurt was so bad, the injustice so unfair, that we eagerly wanted to get revenge, and not just by standing up for ourselves but by hurting the other person.

People sometimes get the wrong idea about revenge. They think it involves some elaborate plot to get even with someone, some movie-worthy master stroke that brings the scales of justice back into balance. Real life is not usually like that. Rather, revenge takes a thousand small forms in our everyday lives—barbed comments aimed at a coworker, gossip behind someone's back in an attempt to sully their reputation, a "See? I told you so" attitude, a wish that someone would fail or learn their lesson. Revenge is at its root a heart attitude that gives rise to all sorts of unpleasant actions and words.

Thankfully, the Bible is very clear about the subject of revenge: Simply put, we have no right to it. We are not allowed to get revenge or even wish revenge on our enemies—not one thought, not one deed, not one sideways comment, not one little prayer that a grand piano would fall on them from a ten-story building. When we get into the forgiveness business, we get out of the revenge business entirely. We cannot do both.

It may seem far-fetched and idealistic that we should not want our enemies to suffer for their actions, but that's the high calling we are aiming for. Stephen, a wonderful servant and the first Christian martyr, was stoned to death for preaching Jesus. While being pummeled with those rocks he used his dying breath to ask the Father to forgive his murderers (see Acts 7). There are many times I can't imagine doing that, but it is what Jesus commanded when He said:

> But I tell you, love your enemies and pray for those who persecute you, that you may be children of your Father in heaven. He causes his sun to rise on the evil and the good, and sends rain on the righteous and the unrighteous.
> —MATTHEW 5:44–45, NIV

Paul echoed this:

> Do not repay anyone evil for evil. Be careful to do what is right in the eyes of everyone.
> —ROMANS 12:17, NIV

When I was a new believer I would read psalms that said things like, "His heart is established; He will not be afraid, until he sees his desire upon his enemies" (Ps. 112:8, NKJV). I loved that. I would pray, "Get 'em, God! Yeah! Kill my enemies and make 'em hurt." Then I saw where Jesus said, "Bless those who curse you, do good to those who hate you, and pray for those who spitefully use you and persecute you" (Matt. 5:44, NKJV). I didn't like that at all. I wanted to rip that page out of the Bible. There is always going to be a temptation to wish bad things on someone who is hurting you or coming against you with attacks that are not true. However, our job is to bless our enemies, pray for those who speak falsely against us, and trust God to be our defense rather than defending ourselves.

Several years ago, I was going through a difficult time, and it was clear that there were some individuals trying to discredit the work of Mercy and myself as the leader. One day I was reading Psalm 112:8 and God showed me that my desire for my enemies should not be that they are annihilated or punished, but instead that they are blessed and set free. He showed me that if I would be faithful to pray for my enemies, He would cause my heart to change toward them so that I could stay in a place of love and compassion rather than anger and bitterness. He reminded me that my struggle is not against flesh and blood, but against the rulers, authorities, and powers of this dark world and against the spiritual forces of evil in the heavenly realms (Eph. 6:12). We often think of people as our enemies, but God reminded me that day that these are people He loves and that I needed to love them as well.

I realized that as I prayed for my enemies, God actually did change the desire of my heart for them. As my heart came more in tune with God's heart, I started getting more of the love of God in my life, and I began asking God to help me see people the way He sees them, to love people the way He loves them. He answered that prayer and a softening took place that surprised even me. What helped me most was when I started praying for people I was really upset with, sometimes through clenched fists and gritted teeth. I would force my mouth to say, "I choose to forgive and I choose to pray for them. I don't feel like praying for them. I don't like them. But I choose to pray for them. I choose by faith to grant forgiveness. I pray for them, Lord, and ask You to open doors of opportunity for them to be blessed." My intensely emotional, negative feelings often melted away within just a handful of days and I started feeling God's compassion for people who had hurt me. The power to forgive is not of ourselves. It is God working in us as we obey in spite of our feelings.

That doesn't mean it is always easy to forgive right away. Sometimes you wrestle through things. Before I started Mercy I worked in child protective services, and when I investigated child abuse cases I came across some of the most horrible characters you could ever meet. They did unimaginable things to children. I was so conflicted because part of me wanted to hurt them—and I mean badly. But as a believer I was supposed to be loving and forgiving. I had to come to grips with what it means that our struggle is not against flesh and blood but against principalities and powers. I had to understand that no human being would do such a thing to a child unless powers of darkness were involved.

Here's where we slam into one of the main stumbling blocks people have when choosing to forgive: Forgiving a person is not saying that what they did to you is OK. Far from it! God actually warns us against calling good evil and evil good (Isa. 5:20). The apostle Paul was very honest about his past life persecuting Christians, and when people persecuted him he called them out on it (Acts 16:37). And the apostle Peter, in every recorded sermon he gave, reminded his hearers that they had wrongly crucified the Author of life.

Forgiving is not saying that what happened is OK. It was *not* OK. God is more grieved and angry about it than you are. Neither does forgiving mean you have to become best buddies and spend vacations together with the person who wronged you. In some cases further contact would be inappropriate and forgiveness will have to take place entirely in your own heart. But at times it is appropriate to call or get together face-to-face and reconcile when you both feel the relationship should continue.

But in all these cases revenge is not your business. It is God's business. The truth is, God's vengeance is a lot scarier than anything we could do. Some people think, "My abuser will never pay for what he (or she) did—I must get revenge for myself." Or, "My husband (or wife) gets away with everything. Someone has to call him out on it." Those are ungodly beliefs; they don't line up with the Word of God, which tells us that we can rest in peace and let God be our vindicator. God promises:

I will deal severely with all who have oppressed you. I will save the weak and helpless ones; I will bring together those who were chased away. I will give glory and fame to my former exiles, wherever they have been mocked and shamed.

—ZEPHANIAH 3:19, NLT

The LORD is slow to get angry, but his power is great, and he never lets the guilty go unpunished.

—NAHUM 1:3, NLT

Do not say, "I'll pay you back for this wrong!" Wait for the LORD, and he will avenge you.

—PROVERBS 20:22, NIV

For he who avenges blood is mindful of them; he does not forget the cry of the afflicted.

—PSALM 9:12, ESV

"Vengeance is Mine. I will repay," says the Lord.

—ROMANS 12:19

One day, on what the Bible calls the day of wrath or the Day of Judgment, we will see God's fearsome, unimaginable anger poured out on His enemies in perfect power and justice. The puny payback you would order for your enemy is nothing compared to that day. The Bible warns that some people are storing up wrath for themselves even now (Rom. 2:5). We read in 1 Thessalonians 4:6, "the Lord is the avenger in all these things, as we also have forewarned you and testified" (see verses 3–8).

God is going to settle the score. In the end, justice will be completely and finally done. So rather than relishing our enemies' future punishment and asking God to go heavy on them now, we must consider the mercy God has given us and the wrath we have been spared by coming to Him. How can people like us, as totally committed followers of Jesus Christ, had all our wrongs dismissed and our sins cancelled out purely by His mercy—how can we wish the worst for any other person? Shouldn't we want others to experience the same liberation from darkness and punishment we have received?

The reality of hell itself should compel us to pray for our enemies. Few, if any of us grasp how indescribably evil and horrible the enemy's ultimate plan for people is. If we each experienced hell for just a few seconds we would be on our knees praying for everyone—those who hurt us, those on death row, the worst people in the world—to come to Christ to avoid that place. When you truly understand the enemy's intentions you want to break agreement with his goal of dragging people to hell and you want the Father to make a way for everyone to live forever with Him—forgiven, just as you and I are.

Jesus warned all of us with a story about this very thing:

Therefore, the kingdom of heaven is like a king who wanted to settle accounts with his servants. As he began the settlement, a man who owed him ten thousand bags of gold was brought to him. Since he was not able to pay, the master ordered that he and his wife and his children and all that he had be sold to repay the debt.

At this the servant fell on his knees before him. "Be patient with me," he begged, "and I will pay back everything." The servant's master took pity on him, canceled the debt and let him go.

But when that servant went out, he found one of his fellow servants who owed him a hundred silver coins. He grabbed him and began to choke him. "Pay back what you owe me!" he demanded.

His fellow servant fell to his knees and begged him, "Be patient with me, and I will pay it back."

But he refused. Instead, he went off and had the man thrown into prison until he could pay the debt. When the other servants saw what had happened, they were outraged and went and told their master everything that had happened.

Then the master called the servant in. "You wicked servant," he said, "I canceled all that debt of yours because you begged me to. Shouldn't you have had mercy on your fellow servant just as I had on you?" In anger his master handed him over to the jailers to be tortured, until he should pay back all he owed.

This is how my heavenly Father will treat each of you unless you forgive your brother or sister from your heart.
—MATTHEW 18:23–35, NIV

We have a very short time to give mercy to others before God's final day. Let's use every day and every hour to offer mercy to people who don't deserve it. God says when we do this we act like Him because "he is kind to the ungrateful and wicked" (Luke 6:35, NIV).

FORGIVING YOURSELF

Some of us may quickly forgive the offenses of others but regret our own poor choices. We may feel safer and more in control by remaining angry with ourselves, but that control is not real and gets eroded quickly. We must learn to extend the same grace we have given others to ourselves. We may feel exposed and vulnerable in the process, but this is the time to rely even more on the Lord's comfort and strength. We can be honest with Him. If we are angry at Him or do not trust Him, we can talk those things out with Him free from guilt or fear. These honest conversations can start the forgiveness process and give a clearer understanding of the Lord's character.

God sent His only Son to this world to die so that we could be free from sin. When we do not forgive ourselves, we are essentially saying that Jesus's death on the cross is not enough for us. God is faithful and just and very gentle with us. In Psalm 103:12 God promises to remove our sin as far as the east in from the west.

Forgiving yourself is no easy task, but the freedom that follows is immeasurable. Trust Him with your hurts and those things you feel so ashamed about—ditch the baggage of shame and receive what God has already done for us.

FORGIVENESS CHANGES THOSE AROUND YOU

When Stephen chose not to lash out at his attackers but rather to intercede for them before God, I believe it unleashed God's grace on the life of a man who participated in Stephen's murder that day: Saul of Tarsus, later known as the apostle Paul. The fact is that your forgiveness may be the key that unlocks someone else's prison. Your forgiveness may catapult your enemy into God's work in a way you never imagined. When you release someone and pray a blessing over them, that's not just nice words; it's powerful. Jesus said, "If you forgive the sins of anyone, they are forgiven them" (John 20:23). In other words, they get to walk in freedom because you released them.

Jesus did this on the cross. He prayed as He hung there, "Father, forgive them, for they do not know what they are doing" (Luke 23:34, NIV). When He breathed His last breath, the centurion in charge of His crucifixion was converted on the spot: "Truly, this Man was the Son of God" (Mark 15:39).

The way you handle unfairness can be a dramatic example for others to follow. It transforms the lives of those around you. It clears the way for the Spirit of God to convict and connect with people, including those who did you wrong.

Let's recap:

- ❃ Forgiveness is not saying that what someone did was OK.

- ❃ Forgiveness is not giving a person permission to hurt you again.

- ❃ Forgiveness does not mean having a relationship with a hurtful person again.

- ❃ Forgiveness does not always mean you have to tell the person you forgive him or her.

- ❃ Forgiveness does not mean that justice will not be done.

Rather:

❄ Forgiveness is saying that what someone did was *not* OK, but that you are letting God bring justice into the situation and defend you. It declares your confidence in His timing and character.

❄ Forgiveness brings you clarity about the relationship and allows you to set boundaries that guard against future harm.

❄ Forgiveness means having a proper heart attitude toward the person and asking God to bless and show mercy.

❄ Forgiveness means trusting that there is a day of judgment coming and leaving people to God's justice, which is much more fearsome and fair than what you or I could order up.

Are you stuck in bitterness about something or someone in your life? I like what a friend of mine says: Forgiveness is not just for big jobs. It's a tool for everyday use, for big and little things. People sometimes use forgiveness on a major hurt but forget to use it when someone is rude in traffic or at the store. I'm here to tell you that forgiveness works up and down the line, from the smallest remark that rubbed you the wrong way to the major disaster perpetrated on you by the enemy through another human being. It's an all-purpose tool. Don't just pull it out for hard stuff. Become an expert forgiver. Get really good at letting things go and offering mercy, for "blessed are the merciful, for they will be shown mercy" (Matt. 5:7, NIV).

Soon forgiveness will come easier and quicker than before, and you will walk in a freedom you have never known.

Chapter 5

KEY #5: BREAKING YOUR FAMILY'S GENERATIONAL PATTERNS

A T THE AGE of twelve I could have told you anything about the men's Vanderbilt basketball team. I was a total sports fanatic. I grew up on a farm in Tennessee, the middle of seven children. Most of my family rooted for the University of Tennessee at Knoxville, but my sister and I fell in love with Vanderbilt sports. I would lie on my bedroom floor with a transistor radio up to my ear and listen to every play of the Vanderbilt men's basketball games. My older sister started making scrapbooks of the Vandy team from articles and photos she clipped from the Nashville newspapers. I followed suit and made similar scrapbooks. They were our heroes.

I also could have told you anything about Mickey Mantle, Yogi Berra, Roger Maris, Bobby Richardson, Whitey Ford, and all of the New York Yankees on the team at that time. I read every sports biography and baseball book I could get my hands on about those guys. When it came to pro football, I was a Dallas Cowboys fan and really admired Tom Landry, Don Meredith, and Roger Staubach. I read the sports pages and every book on football I could find. No romance novels for me—my mind was always on the gridiron, baseball diamond, or basketball court, depending on the season.

My love for sports drove me to work hard to become the best athlete I could be. In junior high and high school I played softball, making the all-star team every year. I also played varsity basketball and ran track. I remember as a kid loving to visit my cousins' house and playing baseball with the neighborhood boys, because they did not know me and I would always get chosen last since I was a girl. I got a kick out of that because I knew I was good enough to impact a game and make them sorry they picked me last. I could hit and throw better than some of the guys! Years later, after I got my college degree and could no longer play sports because of an ACL injury, I went to umpire school and became the first female umpire in Tennessee high school baseball.

People ask me why I'm such a sports fanatic, and the answer is that I had a natural bent for it. But the sad truth is also that sports was an escape from a lot of hurt in our home. My sister Beverly died in a tragic accident on our farm when she was three and a half years old. Unfortunately, my parents both witnessed her death firsthand as she was crushed to death in my father's lap while riding a tractor. When the accident occurred, my dad blamed himself for what happened for the rest of his life. (The full story is told in my book *Mission of Mercy*.)

It was as if all my family members froze emotionally at that point in time. The unspoken family rule was not to talk about anything or express any emotion because it touched the unhealed pain we all felt but never expressed to one another. Looking back, I can see where my parents disconnected from all of us emotionally, possibly out of fear of another loss. It was like everyone shut down and we just stuffed our feelings of grief deeper and deeper.

The calamity of my sister's untimely death threw our family's future and our relationships with one another off course. Nobody came and helped us walk through the grieving process, nor was it ever mentioned. We fended for ourselves emotionally, and rather than coming together, we splintered apart. I would hear my dad at night crying alone, sitting in his chair saying my sister's name over and over. I know now that he was under an oppressive spirit of grief. How I wish someone had come to us and told us, "Jesus bore our grief so we wouldn't have to bear it," but no one did.

Now you can understand why sports was one of the few safe topics of conversation. Enthusiasm over our teams was the closest thing we had to emotional connection. We struck up playful arguments and rivalries while rooting for our teams on Saturdays during college football season, or Sundays watching baseball on the TV in our living room after church.

That's how it was in my family—we shared a legacy of emotional disconnect and unresolved grief. It was a legacy I would have to reckon with later.

DEATH ALL AROUND ME

As I grew older something else happened: a lot of people around me died in accidents. Less than two years after Beverly's death we lost two dear family friends, a mother and son, in a car accident. Less than a year after that our pastor and his wife were killed in a car accident. I had just begun to open up to them about my grief, and now that door to personal healing slammed shut in my face.

Just after high school a guy I had dated and really loved dropped me off one night and went out drinking with friends. His car went over a bridge and he broke his neck, dying instantly.

In college I reconnected with another guy who had been my junior high crush. He asked me out, and I was very willing to see what our future might be, and to tell him all about how I had recently committed my life to Christ. I genuinely cared about him. That weekend he went hiking and died in a climbing accident.

One of my brothers-in-law, Al, was playing golf one Saturday with his buddies and called home to tell my sister, Rebecca, "Keep the kids up. I'll be home in a few minutes to kiss them good night." He never made it. He died at age twenty-nine in a hit-and-run accident that was never solved. This was a deep loss for Rebecca, but also for our entire family. I always told her that if I could meet someone like Al, then I would get married. He was just that special.

Then an aunt died of cancer at a very young age. One of my first cousins died at age twenty-four in a sudden car accident, another first cousin committed suicide at age twenty-six, and another first cousin died of a sudden brain aneurysm. I experienced so much loss that I began to believe that if I got close to someone, something bad would happen to him or her. I now realize that this was a selfish way to think, but nevertheless it was very real to me. It seemed to me that my family had a curse of calamity and tragedy in our bloodline. Nothing else explained the drumbeat of death that followed us. I became afraid of growing close to people for fear of losing them.

Both of those generational patterns—unresolved grief and deadly disasters—left serious scars on my heart that had to be healed properly. Both would come to a head in my life in surprising ways in the future. To avoid getting stuck in life I was forced to deal with each in a godly way.

What Did You Inherit?

All of us inherit patterns of living and thinking that are passed down to us whether we like them or not. The family patterns we inherit can be positive or negative, life-giving or life-destroying. Some family traits give us a great vision for our future. Some threaten to control our lives and even ruin them. Some patterns may be genetic and others behavioral. Some may even have a spiritual component as the enemy empowers harmful habits and emotions.

My family was not just emotionally shut down and plagued by death. In my bloodline I also discovered that my dad's grandfather shot and killed his wife, then shot and killed himself. That alerted me that we had some possible tendencies toward rage in our natural family that I would need to shore up and resist. I haven't tried to kill anybody yet, but my life's not over so you never know. I'm kidding, of course.

What positive or negative patterns do you see in your family history? Are there any obvious life-controlling issues in your family line? Generational patterns can include things like the following:

* Driving career ambition

* Arrogance

* Depression

* A hot temper

* Cynicism

* Difficulty having close relationships

* Substance abuse

* A hard time submitting to authority

* Independence

* Lack of expression of love or affection

The good news is that God has given us the power to identify and reject patterns in our family's history and establish new patterns that bring blessing to our future and our children's futures. We exercise this power when we actively surrender destructive generational patterns to God and work to lay a new foundation in Christ. The Bible clearly says that sinful patterns are less powerful and have a much shorter lifespan than righteous family patterns. God told Moses that those who hate him harm their family line down to the third or fourth generation, but that God shows love "to a thousand generations of those who love [Him] and keep [His] commandments" (Exod. 20:5–6, NIV). Evil can last only a few generations, but those who love God are blessed for a thousand! The Bible confirms elsewhere that "His mercy is on those who fear Him from generation to generation" (Luke 1:50).

The power to change is in your spiritual bloodline. Let me explain. When you were born as a baby you came into a natural, earthly bloodline. You have relatives, shared DNA, a family history, and so on. That has been true of every human being since Adam. Even Jesus had an earthly background through His mother, Mary. His brothers were His real brothers with shared genetics. Jesus did not simply appear from heaven or take the form of a spirit. He arose from the bloodline of David and was just as human as you and me.

It was Jesus's perfect human life that made possible a second birth. God raised Him from the dead in newness of life, with what the Bible calls "the power of an indestructible life" (Heb. 7:16, NIV). Through His blood a new bloodline was created and we too are offered indestructible life. When we come to Christ, we are literally born again by the Spirit. This is not just a nice metaphor or word picture. It is an actual reality. It takes place in the spirit, meaning we cannot see it, but it is more powerful than our earthly bloodline. We literally enter into the family of God through the bloodline of Jesus Christ. His blood is eternal, much stronger than the blood of our earthly families, and has the power to break every evil tendency that comes down to us by genetics or habit.

What kind of Father would God be if He saved us but left us in bondage to what our families have passed down to us—those hurts and habits that threaten to destroy us? No way! He is a good Father, and He provided our way of escape through Jesus Christ. But this bloodline must be chosen by our will to be effective. Just as Jesus offers salvation to everyone but only some receive it to make it actual, so Jesus provides freedom from generational patterns for everyone who is born again—but it only "works" when we appropriate His victory. Galatians 3:13 tells us that "Christ has redeemed us from the curse of the law by being made a curse for us."

In Christ, the curse we may have inherited in generational patterns is broken. He literally became that curse for us. Amazing! Freedom does not come from trying harder or going to support group meetings, though those things can be helpful in their proper contexts. Actual freedom comes through the power of Christ at work in us now because of our inheritance in Him. "He who is in you is greater than he who is in the world," we are assured (1 John 4:4), and that goes for our family patterns as well.

I'm here to tell you that all Christians have access to the power of God's bloodline, which lets us break generational patterns. But so many of us never put it to use! Some of us have a form of religion but essentially deny its power. If I give you a certificate for a four-night stay at a beachside resort, it doesn't do you any good sitting in a drawer. You have to use it. Some people give me gift cards to coffee shops, but if I forget about them and never use them, they will not do me any good. I have to remind myself that the cards are in my purse and pull them out and use them in order to get any benefit from them.

In the same way, we learn to use and appropriate freedom from generational patterns. It's part of renewing our minds and getting God's perspective. It is a deliberate choice supported by our ongoing words and actions. God empowers that choice and rejoices with us as we walk in ever-increasing freedom.

The first step is to recognize the patterns that were handed down to us through our earthly bloodline. At Mercy, the residents learn about generational patterns and are often amazed by how these patterns explain their own family history—why they have fallen into the same cycles of sin that previous family members had. The generational patterns in their lives can be a major part of their bondage. Choosing to pray through and overcome those patterns prevent the patterns from controlling their lives and from being passed down to their own children.

The first step for me and for you is recognizing the patterns we want to resist. We can be aware of areas of family struggle without fearing them. If we don't clearly identify what they are we will never have victory over them. How about you? How have bad family patterns affected you? Do you feel trapped by the choices your father and mother and ancestors made? How have these patterns affected others in your family?

EXPOSE THE PATTERNS

The next step is to bring those patterns into the light, and here is where many people run into a buzz saw. The tendency for every family is to hide bad stuff. They say things such as

- ❀ "It's no big deal."
- ❀ "It's not worth bringing up because it will hurt certain people's feelings."
- ❀ "We've made it this far. Things are fine the way they are."
- ❀ "It's only a problem depending on how you look at it."
- ❀ "Nobody's being hurt anymore. Just forget about it."

Bringing up certain topics in some families unearths major feelings of shame. That's why exposing the patterns can be a volatile but necessary step.

After experiencing so much death among my family and friends, I decided to address the problem head-on. I started earnestly seeking God about why death was so prevalent around me, and I began studying generational patterns. I prayed for God's protection over all my family members and told the enemy he was not allowed to bring calamity and untimely death on us anymore. It felt strange to pray this way because I was one of those who had been taught that everything that happens is God's will. But from that day forward, nobody in my family has experienced an unnatural death. Indeed, some were even spared death in robbery situations where a perfectly functioning gun did not go off when it was aimed right at them. I am convinced that exposing and resisting family patterns broke the string of calamities.

When you expose the devil's plan in your family, your family members may resist you. When I talk about exposing generational patterns I'm not talking about calling a family meeting and shaming everyone. I'm not talking about dishonoring those who came before us. It is very important to seek God about whether to speak or whether to simply pray. Either way, you have authority as a believer to break family patterns and to pray for God's protection over your loved ones.

Also remember that you may have to expose patterns over time as God reveals them to you. It may be a conversation here or there with a relative, or it may just be you dealing with things in your own private prayer life. It may be a process within your own mind of seeing patterns for what they are—not just family quirks but strongholds of the enemy. If the pattern is continuing, perhaps just exposing it in your own mind is the first step to removing its power and helping others get free.

It will take time. In my case, just because untimely deaths stopped happening in my family doesn't mean my mind and my emotions were healed instantly. Rather, my mind had been shaped by those seasons of death and it took me a while to renew it. For some years I was in torment from the enemy who told me that if I got close to anyone the person would die. It wasn't logical but my experience confirmed it. There were times when I was an adult and in full-time ministry that this fear was triggered by someone's behavior.

Let's say I called a close friend and she said, "I'm in a meeting. I'll call you back around nine." If she didn't call back at nine I would wonder if she had been in a wreck. I would even convince myself she was in trouble or dead on the side of some highway. When my friend called me back at ten I would get upset with her and say, "You scared me so bad. Why didn't you call?" She would say, "What's wrong with you? My meeting went late. I called you as soon as I could." Obviously, I was being tormented by damaged emotions that needed to be healed.

Old patterns drive present behavior and can hurt relationships. To bring that weakness of mine into the light I began telling friends about this unnatural fear that would kick in. I asked them to remind me that death was no longer part of my heritage. Letting them know I was overcoming this pattern created understanding in the relationship and freed me of the darkness and isolation I experienced when those fears came back.

Taking Authority Over Your Family Line

Based on the history of mental illness and addiction in her family, Heather thought she was genetically destined to live in despair. She believed her existence was actually a mistake because everything she did or said seemed wrong.

Then she learned about identifying generational patterns that ran in her family and realized that she was no longer doomed to the sins and addictions she was born into. Her family history included things like alcoholism, divorce, gambling, depression, suicide, and sickness. She could observe these habits in many family members. For herself, she decided to take authority over what she received via her bloodline and instead claim the inheritance from her heavenly Father. She chose to make different choices to prevent those family patterns from continuing in her own life. And she affirmed that she is magnificently created by the Creator of the universe and is a victorious, powerful woman of God with a blessed future.

Heather recognized the patterns, exposed them, and then took authority over them.

Once you see the patterns in your family, you can start exercising authority that flows from your spiritual bloodline—straight from heaven itself. For example, my grandfather had a severe case of arthritis and my mother had it as well, and so I confessed over myself all the time, "I'm going to live long on the earth. I will not have arthritis. None of these diseases will be on me."

We had one girl at Mercy whose father had a sex change operation. He came to her graduation dressed like a woman and though it had the potential to be very awkward, we helped her to treat him with honor. The Bible says to honor your father and your mother (Eph. 6:2), despite their lifestyle. We all made the decision to love this girl's father unconditionally, and he was deeply impacted that day at Mercy as he experienced unconditional love from God's people for perhaps the very first time. It also opened the door for him and his daughter to still have a good relationship. Though she did not approve of the fact that her father had a sex change operation, she made the decision to love him unconditionally as was modeled that day by the staff and residents at her Mercy graduation. She also understood that she could pray against this having any impact on her future children.

We have a loving Father in heaven. He is perfect and we are His sons and daughters, meaning we can appropriate all the attributes of God into our own lives. If our mothers and fathers treated each other badly, guess what? We don't have to do the same. We can read that husbands should "love your wives, just as Christ also loved the church and gave Himself for it" and let that be our example (Eph. 5:25). We must identify with our new bloodline, the family of God, the blood of Jesus who overcame all. The Book of Revelation says we triumph by the blood of the Lamb and the word of our testimony (Rev. 12:11). The blood of the Lamb is your inheritance, and it produces the testimony of victory in your life today. It is far greater than the bloodline you were born into naturally.

God said in His Word:

> I give you authority to trample on serpents and scorpions, and over all the power of the enemy. And nothing shall by any means hurt you.
>
> —LUKE 10:19

> "For I know the plans I have for you," declares the LORD, "plans to prosper you and not to harm you, plans to give you hope and a future."
>
> —JEREMIAH 29:11, NIV

> For the grace of God has appeared that offers salvation to all people. It teaches us to say "No" to ungodliness and worldly passions, and to live self-controlled, upright and godly lives in this present age, while we wait for the blessed hope.
>
> —TITUS 2:11–13, NIV

Appropriating the promises of God is not a passive thing. It's like driving a car. That car can get you where you want to go. But just because you drove it to the store yesterday doesn't mean that today it will automatically drive you there on its own. You have to do the work of driving it. That is how we appropriate the promises of God.

You are at the wheel of your life. God has given you directions. Now you make the choice to actively change those family patterns. It might mean resisting anger if anger is part of your family patterns. A practical way to do this that has helped me is to confess God's Word out loud over my own life. For example, as I mentioned before, because anger was a problem in my family, I found a verse in James 1:19 that says I should be quick to hear, slow to speak, and slow to get angry.

If you struggle with sexual sin, it may mean not driving by a bar or a sex shop if those things tempt you. If you struggle with your words, it may mean deliberately speaking kind words to someone who really annoys you. It may mean having an accountability partner for things you struggle with. In time, those areas of weakness can actually become areas of great strength because God's strength is made perfect in weakness (2 Cor. 12:9).

To connect with the bloodline of Christ and claim my new inheritance I spent a lot of time in the Word. I listened to teaching tapes that encouraged and taught me to have faith in God. When I was tempted to fear that someone had died I would fight that fear with the Word and with prayer, the way I did everything else. I spoke truth to replace the lies and the lies lost their power. I learned to trust God with people instead of trying to be in control. I told myself that if someone had died and he or she was a believer, the worst case scenario was that the person was in heaven, and what was wrong with that?

As with everything else in life, it all comes down to choice. A foundational scripture for our ministry and my life is found in Deuteronomy:

See, I set before you today life and prosperity, death and destruction. For I command you today to love the LORD your God, to walk in obedience to him, and to keep his commands, decrees and laws; then you will live and increase, and the LORD your God will bless you in the land you are entering to possess. But if your heart turns away and you are not obedient, and if you are drawn away to bow down to other gods and worship them, I declare to you this day that you will certainly be destroyed. You will not live long in the land you are crossing the Jordan to enter and possess. This day I call the heavens and the earth as witnesses against you that I have set before you life and death, blessings and curses. Now choose life, so that you and your children may live and that you may love the LORD your God, listen to his voice, and hold fast to him. For the LORD is your life, and he will give you many years in the land he swore to give to your fathers, Abraham, Isaac and Jacob.

—DEUTERONOMY 30:15–20, NIV

Ask yourself if in the past you have chosen "death and destruction" or "life and prosperity." What choices can you make now to change the generational patterns in your family?

You recall that my dad was weighed down with grief for the rest of his life after Beverly died. Almost without knowing it, I took that grief upon myself. I was becoming the second generation to mourn unto death, not life, and I didn't even see it. Then my dad caught pneumonia in 2001. In his hospital room the day before he died I still saw the grief in his eyes about Beverly. I was seventeen years into leading Mercy and considered myself someone who was free. But like my dad, I had never grieved in a healthy way for what had happened to our family but had pushed that grief down inside. There it stayed until my dad died—and then it all came rising to the surface. I suddenly felt sad all the time, disconnected from other people, and insecure. I felt overwhelming sadness about losing my dad and about never really having the relationship that a father and daughter should have. Losing Beverly was one thing, and it hurt; but not having a relationship with my father hurt just as much.

I stayed busy to avoid the pain of that loss. I like to take most things head-on, but I sidestepped this pain, hoping it would disappear on its own. Like a lot of ministry leaders I was well-versed in keeping up appearances and saying what I needed to say. I bought into the lie that I needed to be OK for everybody else.

I was speaking at a conference in another country and was attending an evening concert at a big arena. I wasn't speaking this night so I wanted to enjoy the music of one of the biggest bands in Christian music. Twenty thousand people were filling this arena with praise, and yet I sat in the balcony feeling so alone. "I'm a leader. I have to have it all together," I thought. "But I'm hurting as much as anyone here and I don't know how to tell anybody. What's wrong with me?"

I spoke and God blessed the message, but I came home from the conference and knew I needed help. The problem was I didn't know where to turn. Christian leaders are supposed to lead, and I didn't know how to lead myself. I began to see that while you can be anointed to preach in the pulpit or lead a ministry, everyone has to walk out their faith the same way in their personal lives. There are no shortcuts.

Finally, a friend challenged me to get help. "I see you helping all these other people," she said. "What about you?" What I thought would be several sessions of counseling with a Christian counselor turned into seven years. For me, that was the path I needed to take to leave old family patterns behind and fully embrace my inheritance in Christ. I am so thankful for the changes God made in me through it. I'm a different person now—much more compassionate, open, and vulnerable. I didn't realize I had built up walls around my heart trying to protect myself from more pain and loss. Through my counseling process, I realized that my self-made walls to keep out the pain also kept me from the intimate relationships and heart connections that I longed for.

The Bible says, "For I, the LORD your God, am a jealous God, visiting the iniquity of the fathers upon the children to the third and fourth generations of those who hate Me" (Exod. 20:5, NKJV). I believe the enemy tries to come and "visit" every person with generational patterns, to establish them in us. He looks for an entry point, a weak place where he can gain a foothold. But because we are part of a new bloodline, we have the authority to tell the devil, "No way. You are not welcome here. I've got another dad now. I've got another family. Go on and get out of here."

FREEDOM FOR FUTURE GENERATIONS

Being in God's family doesn't mean we should ignore our natural family. Even after disagreements with His brothers and mother, Jesus was able to restore those relationships. His brother James became the head of the church in Jerusalem (see Acts 15), and Jesus made sure His mother was cared for by the apostle John (John 19:26–27). You are part of your natural family for a purpose, and it's not to get a haughty attitude and think, "I'm part of a better family now so I don't have to deal with any of you." The truth is God brought you into His bloodline so you can receive His righteousness as a gift. He is always working to renew and restore His creation.

Joann came to a Mercy home with an unplanned pregnancy. Many in her family all but insisted that she get an abortion. But Joann's heart said no. She decided to have the baby and to raise him herself.

That child is now twelve years old. Joann and the birth father married, bought a house, got jobs, and are planted in a local church. They have amazing stability. Joann's decision to have the baby turned out to be the best thing for her entire family. Her family members apologize to her all the time for encouraging her to abort the child in the womb because they are so in love with her son. He is the joy of that family, and everyone respects Joann for standing up to their poor advice and choosing life. That's how powerful one choice and one life can be.

Just as bad tendencies can be generational, so can freedom. It starts with you. People who choose to stay bound are in essence choosing to enslave their children and grandchildren. Staying bound is selfish. It tells God He's a liar, and it robs the next generation of your godly influence.

We need to flip our perspective on our own pain. Our area of struggle can become our area of greatest power and influence in God. Instead of bemoaning the cards we were dealt, how about thanking God that we get the honor of turning that pattern around? How about thanking God for proving His faithfulness time and again despite our natural family traits and habits?

Today, though I have never been married, I frequently receive cards and e-mails from several hundred men and women in their twenties who call themselves my "grandchildren." They were the babies born to Mercy girls. I was in the labor and delivery room with many of them. They are part of my world today, and are college students and career people. I bump into them wherever I go. I could have moaned and complained that I haven't been married or had kids of my own, but instead I identified with my heavenly bloodline, and the Father has given me more "children" than I could ever have had on my own.

I decided to be free. What you plan and purpose in your heart will flow down through the generations. It's not all about here and now—it's about then and them. Your freedom will affect other people's tomorrows. Your choice to courageously break old patterns and go after that vision of freedom will go far beyond you. Even if you don't have children of your own, you can impact future generations, just as God has allowed me to do through Mercy.

The Bible counsels us:

> Only be careful, and watch yourselves closely so that you do not forget the things your eyes have seen or let them fade from your heart as long as you live. Teach them to your children and to their children after them.
>
> —Deuteronomy 4:9, NIV

> Posterity will serve Him; it will be told to generations about the Lord; they will come and declare His righteousness to a people yet to be born, that He has acted.
>
> —Psalm 22:30–31

Let me pray for you to recognize, expose, and take authority over those family patterns that may have dogged you for too long.

> *Jesus, I ask You to break all harmful and sinful generational patterns in our families and our lives. We choose to forgive our parents and ancestors, releasing any feelings of bitterness or resentment for the consequences their sin had on us. Forgive us, too, for giving in to temptation and yielding to the same kinds of sins. We choose to identify with our spiritual family and the traits of our perfect heavenly Father. Thank You for the new birth! In Jesus's name, amen!*

Chapter 6

KEY #6: THE POWER TO CHOOSE FREEDOM OVER OPPRESSION

As a new Christian I was loving life. I felt such freedom in the Lord. I had new friends, new hopes, and a new peace. So it came as a total shock when I fell into an eating disorder that turned the next five years of my life into a living hell.

It started one night at my pastor's house. He and his wife graciously invited me over to dinner and served rich Southern foods—fried chicken, biscuits and gravy, and sumptuous desserts. I ate a lot that night because the food was so good. I also had committed to clean the pastor's house while he and his wife were at a meeting that night. They left after dinner and I started cleaning the house, but my stomach grew increasingly nauseated. It got so bad that I could hardly stand up. I sat on the bathroom floor and hung my head over the toilet feeling like I was going to throw up any minute, but nothing happened. I thought, "I have got to get this house clean before they get back from that meeting, but I'm so sick I can't even move."

I'm the kind of person who moves heaven and earth so I can keep my word. Now I was stuck. I pictured the pastor and his wife coming home to a dirty house, and me ailing from the food they had served. It just wasn't the scene I wanted. Then it hit me: the only way to feel better so I could finish cleaning the house was to make myself throw up and get the food out of my body. I wasn't even thinking about my weight. I was just determined to keep my commitment. I put my fingers down my throat and induced vomiting. The food came up, the nauseated feeling left, and I felt great relief. I was able to clean the house just as I had promised.

At some point after I had induced vomiting I heard a voice in my head make a practical suggestion. It said, "You can do that all the time and you will never, ever have to worry about your weight. You can eat whatever you want—no limits. Just do this every day."

I didn't know it was the voice of the enemy. I was a new Christian and didn't know how to recognize his voice. The idea of eating whatever I wanted and gaining no weight sounded awesome. Like any young woman, I was weight conscious. The suggestion stuck in my mind, and I pondered it and finally agreed with it. In that moment of agreement I walked directly into a mental and emotional prison.

For the next five years I binged and purged several times a week. Almost immediately I realized it was wrong and I was not in control; the behavior was. My body reacted with severe constipation and a very irregular menstrual cycle. My mind was plagued with guilt as I struggled to stop what I had started. Every time I threw up, I beat myself up emotionally and hated what I was becoming. But I felt helpless. Back then in the 1970s there was very little information about eating disorders. Singer Karen Carpenter had not died of anorexia yet. I had never even heard the word "bulimia." I didn't know other people were experiencing the same thing I was. I just knew I had a big problem.

I had never fallen into substance addiction. Smoking and doing drugs seemed extreme and off-limits in my Christian world. But food wasn't an obvious vice. Everyone had to eat. How could something so commonplace control me? But control me it did. I thought of food constantly—how much I had eaten, when I would vomit it up, how much weight I was gaining, if anyone knew what I was doing, how much I needed to exercise to burn the calories, what possible damage I was doing to my body. It was the worst bondage I have ever experienced. I cried out to God, repented, and fell back into it so many times. I knew that if there were any hope of my being set free, it would be in Christ. How He would release me from this prison, I did not know. I just knew that if I didn't master this thing, it would master me and eventually kill me.

WHEN YOUR CHOICES TAKE YOU CAPTIVE

We have talked much in this book about the choices we make and where they lead us. Just as I opened a door to an eating disorder, some people open doors to various kinds of oppression through their choices. Some of it is deliberate sin. Others fall into it unsuspectingly, as I did. Oppression is slavery to habits, addictions, thought patterns, and even relationships. Severe oppression renders you almost nonfunctional. It feels so heavy and smothering that you can hardly think. It also creates a great deal of fear—"What are people thinking? Do they see this about me? How can I hide it?" People were not created to live under oppression and heaviness, but so many do, and they don't know how to escape it.

Oppression always comes in with our agreement. We may be tricked or deceived, or we may go into it with eyes wide open, but it always involves us opening a door we should not have opened. Inviting oppression is like giving your life away in exchange for nothing. Imagine sitting on your couch and somebody walks into your house, says, "Hey, how ya doin'?" and loads up your TV and your valuables. You wouldn't just sit there and let an intruder steal from you. You would say, "Wait a minute! What are you doing? Get back here with my stuff!" You would call the police because you have a legal right to your possessions.

Yet we so often let the enemy waltz in and take whatever he wants. He steals our peace, torments us, cancels our joy, harms our relationships, and ruins our bodies. We begin to entertain thoughts like, "If I were a better person I wouldn't be struggling with this." "I'm no good." "I'm ugly." "This problem is beyond remedy." "Even God can't help me now. The Bible is nice and all, but it never envisioned what I'm mixed up in." "Even if I kick this habit I will fall right back into it like I have a hundred times before."

Those are deadly lies. I tell you with the force of heaven behind me: you and I can take authority over oppression at any time—including right now. As believers in Christ, we have the power and authority to close doors of oppression in our lives by declaring our authority and commanding oppression to go in Jesus's name. This authority does not come from the power of our personality or will, our cleverness or resolve. No, we are weak but He is strong! Jesus purchased our freedom and legally defeated Satan when He hung on the cross and shed His blood, thus triumphing over sin and death.

In fact, Colossians 2:15 says that "having disarmed principalities and powers, He [Jesus] made a public spectacle of them, triumphing over them in it" (NKJV). Because of the finished work of Jesus at the cross, Satan no longer has a legal right to hold the keys to death, hell, and the grave—he had to hand them over to Jesus (Rev. 1:18). The battle is over! Our victory has been won, but we must use our God-given authority as believers to enforce the enemy's defeat.

Oppression has never been part of God's plan for us! The Bible tells us:

> It is for freedom that Christ has set us free. Stand firm, then, and do not let yourselves be burdened again by a yoke of slavery.
> —GALATIANS 5:1, NIV

I can do all things through Christ who strengthens me.
—Philippians 4:13, nkjv

The Lord also will be a refuge for the oppressed, a refuge in times of trouble. Those who know Your name will put their trust in You, for You, Lord, have not forsaken those who seek You.
—Psalm 9:9–10

Mark 16 tells us that Jesus ascended to heaven and sat down at the right hand of the Father. I believe He sat down because it was our time to rise up and stand against oppression. He delegated His authority to us saying, "It is finished. I'm giving you the keys to the kingdom. Go in My name. These signs shall follow them that believe." We now have authority over any oppression in Jesus's name. That's powerful!

In truth, we don't even need to pray and ask Jesus to release us from oppression. He has already done it and we just need to agree with Him and command the enemy to flee. The Bible says, "No weapon that is formed against you shall prosper" (Isa. 54:17). It says, "For all the promises of God in Him [Christ] are 'Yes,' and in Him 'Amen'" (2 Cor. 1:20).

Just as we open the door to oppression in our lives because of unwise choices we make, as followers of Christ we have the power at any time to tell it to leave. Oppression is like a houseguest: it only stays with your permission. We first must close the doors to the enemy by confession of sin and repentance, and then we have the legal right to command oppression to go. We must let our authority as believers rise up. In Luke 10:19 Jesus said, "Look, I give you authority to trample on serpents and scorpions, and over all the power of the enemy. And nothing shall by any means hurt you." That's freedom language! Let's guard our freedom in Christ as if it's worth millions of dollars because it is worth more than that. It is priceless.

Now let me share with you practical steps to get free and stay free from oppression.

GOING THE OTHER WAY

The first step to gaining freedom from oppression is to confess your sin and truly repent. Repentance literally means to turn around and go the other way. When you do this and walk away from your sins and wrong choices, leaving them under the blood, you tell the enemy he no longer has a legal right to oppress you with that particular oppression. Repenting is not an event; it's a lifestyle. It happens over and over again, not just once. When we genuinely confess the sin and truly walk away from it, we also walk away from whatever stirs up that temptation and oppression in us. For example, if your oppression was lust then you avoid lots of things on the Internet and television. You might cancel your cable TV and have an Internet accountability partner. You don't go to bars and clubs, where sensuality is rampant. You don't drive through sections of town where sexual sin is advertised.

Whatever you need to do, you close the doors to the enemy by confession of sin and repentance as I mentioned previously. Only then do you have the legal right to command the oppression to go. Then, when the enemy comes back to try to tempt you with that oppression again, you can stand up to him and say, "No. I will not allow this torment to come back. I've closed the door and I will not re-open it."

My friend Susan comes from Dutch and Scottish backgrounds and recognized a lot of rebellion and pride in her family patterns. One day she had an argument with her husband and noted more than a little rebellion in her response. She thought, "Whoa, that's rebellion. I'm not having that take over my life. Rebellion, you're not welcome anymore. I repent of that and choose not to entertain those feelings anymore. In Jesus's name, leave." There was no big flash of lightning, no dramatic feeling, but things changed. Rebellion did not rise up in her so fast anymore, and peace and gentleness took over instead.

Susan knew the power of authority. There are times to get loud with the devil, but a whisper can do just as much damage to the kingdom of darkness. Authority is authority. No drama is needed to activate it. You can breathe the name of Jesus, and all of heaven stands with you.

SUBMITTING TO GOD

Once we make the legal decision to evict the devil and his oppression, we resist him, as Susan did. Many people know the verse in James that says, "Resist the devil, and he will flee from you" (James 4:7). But they are quoting only the second half of the verse. Resisting only works after you do what James says right before: "*Therefore submit yourselves to God.* Resist the devil, and he will flee from you" (v. 7, emphasis added).

The order of this is critical: submit to God first, then resist the devil and he will flee. What does submitting to God mean? It means aligning our lives with the way He wants us to live in every area. It doesn't mean perfection but rather a sincere commitment to please Him and to obey wholeheartedly. If our decision to close the door on past oppression is halfhearted, and we leave it cracked open just in case serving God isn't what we hoped it would be, we may as well give the devil the keys again. I said it before: God wants us all in. To walk with God in freedom we must set our minds permanently on things above, not on things of this earth. Remember, we are dead, and our lives are hidden with Christ in

God (Col. 3:3). To submit to God means shutting the door permanently. Only then will resisting the devil work.

We must also recognize that our lives are knit together into one piece. Every part of our lives affects the other. If we decide to evict an oppressive habit or thought pattern but hold on to known sin in other areas of life, the devil will eventually try to exploit those sinful openings to make a mess of everything. For example, if you submit to God in the area of lust but hold on to your fiery temper and unkind tongue, or to unresolved hurts, those bad habits and hurts will weaken your resolve in all areas.

Sin is corrosive. Like battery acid, it can leak everywhere and harm your whole life. The good news is that the principles of freedom and strength work together the same way, but in a positive direction. The freedom you find by submitting to God by, say, forgiving others, will strengthen your resolve to walk free of envy or lust or what have you. I'll remind us that the principles of freedom are not so much steps in a particular sequence as a whole lifestyle. They knit together and support each other like a tapestry. The bottom line is that submitting to God means submitting in all areas of life. When we do this as best we can, with a sincere commitment, the Holy Spirit empowers our choice.

I warn you that the devil will come back at strategic times to try to put that old oppression back on us. The Bible says that when the devil was finished tempting Jesus in the desert, the devil left him "until an opportune time" (Luke 4:13, NKJV). When the devil leaves, he's always looking over his shoulder for a way to come back. It happened to me with the sudden onset of an eating disorder, and it happened to Allison, who now works at Mercy with us. Before she met the Lord, Allison looked to worldly pleasures for fulfillment—attention from the opposite sex, partying, drinking, even experimenting with drugs in college. She grew up in a non-Christian home until her mom received Christ when Allison was in high school.

In college Allison joined a sorority and became promiscuous. She didn't have a good relationship with her father, and that lack of fatherly love and support led her to seek fulfillment in relationships with guys. She thought she was safe going with the flow of what everyone else was doing, but it only brought misery. When her boyfriend broke up with her, Allison bottomed out emotionally. Facedown on the floor one night, she recalled her mom's commitment to Christ and cried out to the Lord for help. She gave her life to Christ, but the devil was already fashioning a snare for her future.

Not long after Allison began following Jesus, her mom developed cancer. Within two years her mom was dead, and Allison's life was turned upside down. She had not put down strong roots in the Lord when she moved back home from college. There, with old friends and old patterns around her, she fell into drinking and the party lifestyle again. She was exposed to pornography through a relationship she was in, though she knew it was wrong and not God's design. She was desperate to be loved and accepted. With her mother gone, Allison felt so alone.

The images of what she had seen and done did not go away. They lay dormant in her mind even as Allison got back on track and committed herself anew to Christ. She met a wonderful young man and they got married. During their courtship Allison shared about her past and held nothing back. But after she got married, she found that some of the images she had seen seemed to be burned into her brain. She knew she should feel wonderful and free now that she was forgiven and clean before the Lord, but nobody had told her that looking at explicit images and participating in certain behaviors would be hard to forget—and that the devil would use them to try to wreck her godly relationship with her husband.

Allison's heart was broken and she realized then the damage she had done to her mind in those years—damage to her purity and self-image. Before she got married, the Lord was faithful to renew her and tell her she was spotless before Him, but Allison and her husband had to work through the struggle she was having. She learned the hard way that when you have a promiscuous past or some other sinful lifestyle, the effects don't always surface until you find your lifelong mate and ministry partner. The enemy knew Allison's weak spot was forgiving herself for what she had done. He threatened to drag her into a new kind of oppression of guilt and shame. She had to learn to see herself through the Lord's eyes.

"I'm so passionate in my love for Christ that it was heart-breaking that I had messed up myself and others and wasted that time," Allison says. "Having regrets is hard. Of course my husband is the perfect fit for me. He never held my past against me or made me feel less than the best. Also, having my husband pray the Word over me out loud was very helpful. When I see girls choosing the path of sexual sin, I want to say, 'This is not worth it. Please. You don't know how the enemy will use having sex before marriage to mess you up.'"

Allison and her husband overcame by reading the Word, declaring God's truth and promises over their lives, and shutting the door to thoughts and images that brought up old wounds. They limit what they put before their eyes. For example, they choose not to watch certain PG-13 movies because they depict too much implied sex. They want to wholeheartedly glorify the Lord and not stray into anything that brings up issues in their marriage. Allison calls it knowing their boundaries in the Lord. For them, as for all of us, submitting to God and shutting the door on oppression means tailoring life in a way that's specific to our situation and struggles.

IDENTIFYING THE ENEMY'S VOICE

The enemy found a foothold in Allison's life and exploited it as best he could. At the time, Allison didn't know she was doing anything bad. She was simply enticed. The Bible says "each person is tempted when they are dragged away by their own evil desire and enticed. Then, after desire has conceived, it gives birth to sin; and sin, when it is full-grown, gives birth to death" (James 1:14–15, NIV). It also tells us, "No temptation has taken you except what is common to man. God is faithful, and He will not permit you to be tempted above what you can endure, but will with the temptation also make a way to escape, that you may be able to bear it" (1 Cor. 10:13).

If we have not been trained to know right and wrong, how can we tell the difference between the enemy's voice and God's voice? With practice and by observing the fruit. When you obey a thought or suggestion that leads to harm, you begin to recognize that voice as evil. When you obey the voice that leads to joy and peace—that's the Holy Spirit. The Bible tells us it is not difficult for a sincere follower of Christ to distinguish between them. It should begin to come naturally even when we are young in the faith. Jesus said, referring to Himself, "To him the doorkeeper opens, and the sheep hear his voice. He calls his own sheep by name, and he leads them out. When he brings out his own sheep, he goes before them. And the sheep follow him, for they know his voice" (John 10:3–4). Sheep don't need a lot of training to learn the good shepherd's voice. The prophet Isaiah confirmed this when he said, "Whether you turn to the right or to the left, your ears will hear a voice behind you, saying, 'This is the way, walk in it'" (Isa. 30:21). Jesus further promised that "the Counselor, the Holy Spirit, whom the Father will send in My name, will teach you everything and remind you of all that I told you" (John 14:26). John wrote, "As for you, the anointing you received from him remains in you, and you do not need anyone to teach you. But as his anointing teaches you about all things and as that anointing is real, not counterfeit—just as it has taught you, remain in him" (1 John 2:27, NIV).

Here are some simple ways I have found to recognize God's voice:

1. He always speaks in agreement with His Word. He will not tell you to watch pornography or have sex with your fiancée. He will not speak to you in contradiction to his written Word.

2. His voice is gentle and sometimes soft. He does not pressure us but always leaves an element of choice. My friend Debbie Harvie shared with me a great analogy: the difference between goat herders and shepherds is that goat herders drive goats from behind through intimidation and pressure, whereas sheep are led by the shepherd's voice. If you feel driven and pressured, it is not God's voice. If you feel a sense of peace, empowerment, and choice, that is God's voice.

3. God will speak to you through other means to confirm what He is saying. When you ask a Christian friend or pastor for wisdom, God often will use that person to affirm what He has told you. The Bible says that "by the testimony of two or three witnesses every word may be established" (Matt. 18:16).

4. Circumstances also will confirm what God is speaking.

Here are ways to identify the enemy's voice:

1. His suggestions often seem too good to be true.

2. He often speaks a mixture of truth and deception, which brings confusion and conflicted feelings about what he is suggesting.

3. He clearly goes against God's Word.

4. His idea is centered on your gratification.

5. It doesn't line up with your circumstances or the advice godly people are giving to you.

If you choose to follow the right voice, the Holy Spirit will wonderfully encourage and enable you to walk that way. If you choose the voice of self-gratification, the enemy will be there egging you on. Every choice is empowered either by God or the enemy. It all starts with you choosing which voice to follow.

When Stacy was eight years old, her world turned upside down when her mom died of leukemia. She began to feel an overwhelming burden of guilt for things she thought she could have done to make her mom's life easier. She even convinced herself that she had played a part in her mom's death.

Stacy accepted the suggestion that she was partially responsible for her mother's death and began to drive herself toward perfection. She exercised obsessively and posted exercise routines all over her bedroom walls. She spent hours a day focusing on her perceived physical imperfections. To compensate for feeling overweight she limited herself to one meal a day. Eventually, she would not eat for days at a time, all while exercising and taking diet pills and caffeine pills to get through the day.

Soon she was so thin that she had to hide her body under baggy clothes. She wore boys' pants a few sizes too big and loose

T-shirts. Friends at school noticed her strange eating habits and called her out on it, but Stacy refused to admit she had a problem. Soon, her teachers noticed her lack of weight and saw a difference in her attitude that resulted from the lack of nutrition, diet pills, and overexercising. Stacy started to pass out unexpectedly and lose large amounts of hair from being so malnourished. Her family was afraid and unsure of what to do, so they did nothing.

Stacy had been a Christian for years but was more devoted to losing weight than to developing her relationship with God. The eating disorder took all her time and energy. She essentially submitted to it and invited a heavy weight of oppression. At times she actually ignored God because she thought He would make her gain weight or keep her from losing weight. She knew He wanted what was best for her, but she wanted to be in control. She didn't fully appreciate that when we do not submit to God, we submit to the devil and give him control.

Stacy finally decided to get well and came to a Mercy home. There she gave her wounded heart over to God and let Him mend it with His love. She had a lot of forgiving and healing to do, but it didn't take long for her to give up her old mentality and walk in the authority God meant for her to have. The enemy had empowered Stacy's choice to become obsessed with her weight, but by choosing to surrender control, follow healthy habits, and let God shape her lifestyle, Stacy experienced a dramatic turnaround.

A choice, followed by God's empowerment—that is God's plan for your freedom, just as it was with Stacy. We are not in this alone. The Bible says:

> But you belong to God, my dear children. You have already won a victory over those people, because the Spirit who lives in you is greater than the spirit who lives in the world.
>
> —1 JOHN 4:4, NLT

Look, I have given you authority over all the power of the enemy, and you can walk among snakes and scorpions and crush them. Nothing will injure you.

—LUKE 10:19, NLT

For I am convinced that neither death nor life, neither angels nor demons, neither the present nor the future, nor any powers, neither height nor depth, nor anything else in all creation, will be able to separate us from the love of God that is in Christ Jesus our Lord.

—ROMANS 8:38–39, NIV

Put on the whole armor of God, that you may be able to stand against the wiles of the devil. For we do not wrestle against flesh and blood, but against principalities, against powers, against the rulers of the darkness of this age, against spiritual hosts of wickedness in the heavenly places. Therefore take up the whole armor of God, that you may be able to withstand in the evil day, and having done all, to stand. Stand therefore, having girded your waist with truth, having put on the breastplate of righteousness, and having shod your feet with the preparation of the gospel of peace; above all, taking the shield of faith with which you will be able to quench all the fiery darts of the wicked one. And take the helmet of salvation, and the sword of the Spirit, which is the word of God; praying always with all prayer and supplication in the Spirit, being watchful to this end with all perseverance and supplication for all the saints.

—EPHESIANS 6:11–18, NKJV

The weapons we fight with are not the weapons of the world. On the contrary, they have divine power to demolish strongholds.

—2 CORINTHIANS 10:4, NIV

They overcame him by the blood of the Lamb and by the word of their testimony, and they loved not their lives unto the death.

—Revelation 12:11

Set Free on New Year's Eve

Five years into my struggle, on New Year's Eve, after repenting and failing so many times, I got on my face and said, "God, I'm not moving from this spot until You break this yoke of bondage off of me." My friends wanted me to go out with them but I refused. I had to meet with God and determine my future.

I stayed on my face the whole night and begged the Lord, "Tell me what to do to be free from this. I know it's not Your will for me to stay in captivity. Help!" I grabbed on to the promise in Jeremiah 33:3—"Call to Me, and I will answer you, and show you great and mighty things which you do not know"—and held on for dear life.

That night God met me. He said I had become fearful of food. In an effort to lose weight I was exercising a great deal and eating very little. Yet I was still gaining weight. Despite my binging and purging, I actually weighed more than when I had started. Everything the enemy had told me was a lie, and I had gotten myself into a bondage of fear of eating.

Then God communicated the truth of what I was going through by way of a vision. In it I saw a fireplace. One of my favorite things to do when I was a girl was to visit my grandfather's house, where he had a big fireplace. He would bring in logs, put them on the fire, and watch it roar and roar. Because the fire was so robust, the logs would catch fire and burn very quickly.

God showed me that roaring fire and said, "That's how a healthy metabolism is supposed to look. Your body is designed to burn food, and if you don't keep eating, that fire goes out. Because of what you've done to your body, your metabolism is like a fire at the end of the night with little embers. When you put a log on it, the embers may char the wood a bit but the log will just sit there. You have ruined your metabolism and it no longer burns things up. That's why every time you eat something you gain weight."

It all seemed so clear. I had been fighting my body, and my body had been fighting back. I was ruining my health and devastating my confidence and peace.

Now I knew what the problem was, and I asked God for the solution. He told me very simply, "Eat when you're hungry. Listen to your body—it will tell you what it needs. Eat regular meals and don't overeat. Your body will burn the food off. Walk three or four times a week for an hour, and don't weigh yourself anymore." His instructions were so basic that it reminded me of Jesus's promise that His yoke is easy and His burden is light. I had turned my life into a maze of rules and restrictions that were running me ragged. His way was so much simpler and better.

I took Him at His word and gave the outcome to Him. "OK, God," I said. "I'm going to do exactly what You told me to do." I found a friend who would walk with me a few times a week. I stopped weighing myself and counting calories. Right away everything started changing in my body and mind. I felt great peace and freedom. The fear was gone. I didn't have to think all the time about exercise or eating. My health was restored and my body felt good.

Then a surprising thing happened. I noticed that my clothes were getting way too big for me. I was a size ten the day I began to follow God's plan. In one year I went from a size ten to a size four and have been that way ever since. That was well over thirty years ago. It took no stringent exercise. All I did was walk three or four times a week for an hour—walked, not ran. If I craved a hamburger, I ate one. If I craved a candy bar, I ate it and it satisfied me. These days I eat healthier items, but I don't restrict myself on account of fear of gaining weight. The truth is I didn't know what size I would become and I didn't care. I just believed God's prescription and followed it in obedience. Whatever happened was fine with me. I want to be clear that I am not talking about a weight loss plan, and weight loss was not my goal. My goal was to escape the oppression and stop being controlled by fear. I aimed for total obedience to what God revealed to me and left the outcome entirely to Him. Through that I learned that when we follow God's path of freedom He takes care of us, body and soul. We can leave all the results to Him, as the good Father He is.

God heard the cry of my heart and set me free from bondage. If you are struggling as I was with an eating disorder or something else that has you in chains, I encourage you to follow the real-world advice I'm giving you in this chapter and do what I did: call out to God for specific wisdom about your situation. He will answer!

Let's review those biblical principles for getting free of oppression:

1. Confess the area of sin. Be specific. There is power in being specific. It shines a light in all the dark places and lets the enemy know he can't hide anywhere.

2. Repent—turn and walk the other way daily. Don't justify wrong behavior. Treat it like a snake that has fastened itself to your hand and shake it off into the fire.

3. Submit to God. As far as you are concerned, every area of your life should be under His control. If He shines a light on a certain area where you are still harboring darkness, confess and repent of it quickly.

4. Resist the devil. Having submitted your whole life to God, you have authority to command the devil to leave. What an awesome thing! Tell him to get lost and leave you alone.

5. Walk in freedom and don't let the enemy come back "at an opportune time" to revisit you with oppression. Build the strength of total commitment into all areas of your life for great stability.

God loves you and does not want you to live in the nightmare and heartache of oppression any longer. You will get free, and I trust you will share your testimony with us at Mercy so we can rejoice with you.

Next we will look at how to sustain freedom and victory in your life over the long term.

Chapter 7

KEY #7: HOW TO MAINTAIN LIFELONG FREEDOM

I COULD NOT HAVE been more excited about the first job I landed as I was completing my college education. As athletic director at a correctional facility for three hundred teenage girls, I thought about all of the cool opportunities I would have to interact with them on a daily basis. In this particular role, my job was to organize intramural sports and plan all of the campus activities inside the walls of the girls' prison. The cool part of my job is that I saw every single girl every single day because state law mandated that they have daily exercise.

As a committed Christian, I looked for opportunities to speak life into incarcerated teens who felt desperate and hopeless. Besides that, since I was such a sports fanatic, I loved the idea of organizing intramural softball, basketball, volleyball, and so on. We even had an indoor swimming pool, a gym with a basketball court, and a game room with all kinds of games, including an air hockey table. I even had the privilege, as state funds were made available, of facilitating the building of a softball field on the back side of the campus, as well as an outdoor skating rink and circular bicycle track. It was a very large campus with lots of buildings, and I had a heart to make it as fun as I possibly could because I genuinely cared about the girls.

The cool part about doing intramural sports with all the young women was that I was able to see how talented some of them really were. I got the idea to go to the prison warden and ask if I could take the best players in both basketball and softball and join the city league. I really thought we could be competitive, and after much thought the warden agreed to give it a try, but also cautioned me that if there were issues, she would have to take a second look at it.

With that we were off and running. I formed a team of the very best players, and we signed up to participate in both city league basketball and softball.

Though I was very competitive and wanted to win, my goals went beyond that. I found that playing sports together encouraged the girls to drop their barriers and connect at a heart level with one another. Sports taught them valuable life skills and teamwork. They opened up to me more than ever about their lives, and in some cases I was able to share my faith and talk about the reality of how Christ had changed my life. However, I was still very tough on them in practice because I was so passionate about winning. If they were lazy I made them run extra laps.

The results of our hard work paid off. In our first season we came in second place in the city league. We had some natural athletes on the team, and some girls could hit the ball a mile. I knew going into the second season that we had a good chance to win it all.

By the end of the second season we were really cooking, tied for first place with the best team in the league. Finally, it came down to a championship game. One afternoon we boarded the bus marked Tennessee Correctional System, with guards carrying mace traveling with us for security reasons as usual. Already dressed in our uniforms, we were heading to a city park to play the championship game at night under the lights.

The game got off to a good start. The other team was strong, but we held our own. We seemed almost evenly matched. I was hopeful that our girls could dig deep and pull out a victory. By the bottom of the last inning we were behind by just one run. One of our girls got on first base with no outs, and one of our strongest hitters came up, putting the potential winning run at the plate.

"Rally time," I thought. "This is going to happen. We're really going to get a chance to win."

Our hitter looked at a pitch or two, then smacked the ball all the way to the right field fence. It bounced off the fence as our dugout erupted with cheers. Standing in the coach's box at third base, I kept one eye on the ball and waved the runner from first base home to score. Now it was tied, and the other team's right fielder was bobbling the ball. It was an almost-certain inside-the-park home run. We were about to win the entire city league championship!

I waved my arm like a windmill to signal for the hitter, who was rounding second base, to keep up her speed and head home for the winning run. But as she came around second I noticed that she wasn't coming into third base at the correct angle. Instead she was coming straight at me. "What's going on?" I wondered. "Is she confused?" Nevertheless, she kept coming straight at me as the right fielder finally got hold of the ball and prepared to throw it home.

Our girl came trucking toward me, closer and closer. I wondered what she was going to do and how she would make the turn to home plate. It almost seemed like she would plow me over. Suddenly, when she reached third base, instead of rounding toward home she veered in the opposite direction and took off running. Before I knew it she had jumped a fence and was heading for freedom. The guards immediately started chasing her. The rest of us could only watch her disappear into the night.

The game was called immediately. The guards radioed the city police for backup but couldn't find the girl that night. She was a very fast runner and had a pretty good head start on them. The next day they found her and brought her back to the correctional facility to spend thirty days in solitary confinement. Her shenanigans had caused us to forfeit the game just seconds before winning. I knew I would see this girl face-to-face because part of my job was to provide daily recreational activity for any girl placed in solitary confinement. When we came face-to-face for the first time since she bolted, I was fuming. "Girl, the least you could have done was to cross home plate before you took off!" I said. Everything we had worked for as a team to win the championship was lost the moment she made that decision. It took me a while to forgive her.

That girl reminds me of some people in life who decide to walk the path of freedom. They come to the plate, get a great hit, and start rounding the bases. But on the cusp of victory they decide to run the other way, fleeing back to old lifestyles and habits, and thinking somehow things will improve. As that girl discovered, there was no freedom going back to what you were mixed up in before. Victory is ahead, not behind. If you are sincerely following Christ and taking the advice in this book then you have joined the winning team. You are already walking in freedom. This is no time to get spooked and run the opposite way. Paul exhorted the Galatian church, which was straying from the truth, "You were running a good race. Who cut in on you to keep you from obeying the truth?" (Gal. 5:7, NIV).

At Mercy, though we have most girls for an average of six months, we are equipping them for lifelong success from day one. We are a lot less concerned with their progress at week two than we are at year two and year ten and year twenty-five. We are relentlessly focused on preparing them to maintain lifelong freedom. I feel the same way about you who are reading this book. After you set this book down, how are you going to live it out? Let me share with you some of the key lifestyle habits that help our Mercy girls and many other people maintain freedom for life.

We'll start with what we call the Four Stay-Ins:

1. Stay in prayer.

2. Stay in the Word.

3. Stay in church.

4. Stay in fellowship with other believers.

STAY IN PRAYER

Prayer means more than bowing your head and reciting your needs to God. It means more than giving Him praise and adoration. It goes further than pouring out your true emotions to Him, though these are all good things. Prayer is the essence of your personal relationship with God. It is to your spiritual life what breathing is to your physical life. It is turning your attention to God and talking with Him throughout the day, acknowledging Him in all your ways.

These conversations with God can be planned and put on your calendar, just as you might plan time with a spouse or friend. These are what are commonly referred to as devotional times. Other prayers happen moment-by-moment. Paul called it praying "without ceasing" (1 Thess. 5:17). These short, quiet conversations with God combined with regular times to sit and listen to His voice connect you to God in a powerful way.

Ongoing dialogue with your Creator is not just a nice, spiritual idea—it's the foundation for the Christian life. Just believing the right things is not enough. Jesus said He would one day tell people who believed they were His followers, "I never knew you. Depart from Me" (Matt. 7:23). He didn't say, "Depart from Me because you believed some wrong things about Me" or, "Depart from Me because you didn't do enough for Me." He said He didn't "know" them, meaning He did not have a vital relationship with them. The basis of relationship is communication, and that starts with simply talking to God.

Some people have the mind-set that God is going to do whatever He wants no matter if we pray. That is total baloney. Our prayers are not futile; they matter to God. In the throne room of heaven, where the Father sits in glory, guess what permeates the atmosphere before Him? The prayers of people like you and me. That simple thing we say to God while driving in the car or between meetings or before bed is a beautiful fragrance to Him. Friend, God loves to hear from you! He is relational by nature. Though invisible to us now, He hears us. He cares, and He answers. Prayer changes the course of human history. Prayer changes your life. Prayer changes your heart.

I believe it's possible, even probable, that at the end of our lives the number one regret of most believers will be that we did not spend more time with God in this ongoing conversation called prayer. Prayer is intimate friendship with God, and intimacy with God can take on a variety of forms. Sometimes it is laughter, sometimes tears. Sometimes it's listening to His wisdom or just being in His presence. Sometimes it is praise, or forcefully placing our petitions in front of Him and asking for intervention. Sometimes it is venting our grievances and emotions about daily life. Prayer is a thousand things, a journey that makes you more childlike and relaxed even as you grow more mature and loving. It is a relationship so precious that it's a wonder more people don't give it greater priority.

If we stay in prayer, half our battles will be won. God will give you guidance for the other areas of your life. He will tell you who your friends ought to be, what to say when talking with people, where to work, where to live, where to vacation, and how to serve others. One of the biggest decisions of our lives is, Will you be a man or woman of prayer? Or will you simply take the benefits of salvation and turn to God only when you feel the need? That one decision will define who you are more than almost any single decision you make. It matters more than whom you marry, how you raise your kids, where you work, what kind of shape you're in, where you went to college, where you go to church, where you live, and so on. Prayer changes every situation and every life circumstance.

Consider the passages below as you commit to a life spent in personal dialogue with God:

> And without faith it is impossible to please God, for he who comes to God must believe that He exists and that He is a rewarder of those who diligently seek Him.
>
> —HEBREWS 11:6

> Pray in the Spirit always with all kinds of prayer and supplication. To that end be alert with all perseverance and supplication for all the saints.
>
> —EPHESIANS 6:18

> Be anxious for nothing, but in everything, by prayer and supplication with gratitude, make your requests known to God. And the peace of God, which surpasses all understanding, will protect your hearts and minds through Christ Jesus.
>
> —PHILIPPIANS 4:6–7

> Trust in the LORD with all your heart, and lean not on your own understanding; in all your ways acknowledge Him, and He will direct your paths.
>
> —PROVERBS 3:5–6

"When the Spirit of truth comes, He will guide you into all truth. For He will not speak on His own authority. But He will speak whatever He hears, and He will tell you things that are to come. He will glorify Me, for He will receive from Me and will declare it to you."

—John 16:13–14

In the morning, Lord, you hear my voice; in the morning I lay my requests before you and wait expectantly.

—Psalm 5:3, niv

I will stand at my watch and station myself on the watch-tower; and I will keep watch to see what He will say to me, and what I will answer when I am reproved.

—Habakkuk 2:1

"Call to me and I will answer you and tell you great and unsearchable things you do not know."

—Jeremiah 33:3, niv

God loves to hear your voice! Call to Him consistently and with expectation that He will respond. Your life will radically change for the better.

Stay in the Word

The other primary way we interact with God is through His Word. Imagine that a bank owner brought you to a vault buried deep in the bank; unlocked the huge, heavy door; swung it open; and invited you to walk through and take whatever you wanted. There you found countless stacks of bills, gold, silver, diamonds, jewelry, stock investments, and more, all for the taking. God has done just that with His Word. He has given us an endless vault of knowl-edge about Himself in these inspired teachings and historical records. He expects us to go after it with the same fervency that we would stuff our pockets with valuables in that bank vault.

Proverbs 2:3–5 tells us, "Yes, if you cry out for knowledge, and lift up your voice for understanding, if you seek her as silver, and search for her as for hidden treasures, then you will understand the fear of the LORD, and find the knowledge of God." The Bible also tells us, "It is the glory of God to conceal a thing, but the honor of kings is to search out a matter" (Prov. 25:2). Freedom does not arrive passively at your doorstep like a package you ordered online; you get it by diving in and pulling the most out of God's Word with energy and passion.

- ❈ God instructs us through His Word.

- ❈ God speaks directly to our life situations through His Word.

- ❈ God sustains our very lives through His Word.

- ❈ God gives the wisdom we need every day to do and say what pleases Him by His Word.

Let me ask, what did you eat for breakfast, lunch, and dinner on July 28? Do you have any idea? Probably not, but those three meals kept you alive that day. In the same way Jesus said, "It is written, 'Man shall not live by bread alone, but by every word that proceeds out of the mouth of God'" (Matt. 4:4).

We need to realize that just as important as it is for us to daily feed our bodies, it is even more important for us to daily feed our souls. We often place the Bible to the side or hope we get enough on Sunday to take us through the week, but God's Word is not a dessert, snack, or optional course—it is the main course. It is what sustains us. Jesus said, "If you remain in My word, then you are truly My disciples. You shall know the truth, and the truth shall set you free" (John 8:31–32).

Jesus connected abiding in His Word to being free. Look at it this way: there is no freedom without abiding in His Word. We can talk the talk and shout the shout and proclaim and declare freedom all we want. If we're not abiding in the Word, it isn't going to happen.

Thankfully, the more of God's Word we consume and hide in our hearts, the freer we will be. It's a rock-solid promise. Why? Because God's Word "is alive, and active, and sharper than any two-edged sword, piercing even to the division of soul and spirit, of joints and marrow, and able to judge the thoughts and intents of the heart" (Heb. 4:12). In other words, the Word of God powerfully works in us to sustain freedom in Christ, judging and removing wicked thoughts so we can walk in newness of life, unencumbered by past failures and sin. Amen!

God's Word has another very practical benefit: it gives our minds something to focus on. Some people commit to overcoming certain struggles but spend most of their time thinking about the struggle. That's a big mistake. Whatever you look at begins to fill your field of vision. Whatever you dwell on becomes your destination. How many times have you been driving and you looked in a certain direction only to find your car drifting quickly toward what you were looking at? It's called visual-directional control. Fighter pilots use it to steer their jets. Wherever you look, that's where you will end up.

You cannot go in two directions at once. When you fill your eyes with God's Word, looking "into the perfect law of liberty" (James 1:25), it automatically takes your eyes off other things and you naturally move in that direction. If you are going in the direction of His Word, you can't be going in the wrong direction. Filling your mind with God's Word pushes out destructive and unhelpful thoughts. So set your thoughts on God every morning when you wake up. Read the Word right away. Give it priority over social media and e-mail and even other people in your household.

Incorporate praise and worship into your life. Go outside and admire His creation. God's Word gives our minds something to rest on, to consider, to marvel at, to be convicted by. If we let it, God's Word will shape our words, behavior, thoughts, and friendships—everything about us. It's a much better way to live. Philippians 4:8 says, "Whatever things are true, whatever things are noble, whatever things are just, whatever things are pure, whatever things are lovely, whatever things are of good report, if there is any virtue and if there is anything praiseworthy—meditate on these things" (NKJV).

There is no more powerful combination of life habits than praying and reading God's Word. These days there are so many ways to study the Word. Books by my friends Joyce Meyer, Neil Anderson, and Beth Moore are great resources. You can join a group Bible study and also do an individual study. I encourage both. For less than what it costs to fill your tank with gas you can buy a year's worth of Bible study resources that will dramatically change your life. If you spend the next six months in consistent prayer and reading the Word, I can guarantee you, it will transform your life. If you already pray and read the Word consistently, set a new goal and go deeper and further in God than you have ever been. The landscape of your life will change. You will experience in an ongoing way the "freedom we have in Christ Jesus" (Gal. 2:4, NIV). The Bible promises, "You [God] will keep him in perfect peace, whose mind is stayed on You, because he trusts in You" (Isa. 26:3).

STAY IN CHURCH

Trish, who walked through a dark passage when she found herself facing divorce and alone with a young daughter, made a really good decision: "I never checked out from church," she says. "I was raised that your relationship with the Lord is the first priority."

She stayed rooted in a strong community of people who supported her. In practical ways they stepped in to cook meals, clean her house, and do laundry when Trish couldn't. Some friends would pick up her daughter from school and take her to doctors' appointments. Trish knew she could count on them. She felt the love of the body of Christ in a tangible way.

Trish also found purpose and direction in her church community. She was invited to run the single mothers' ministry, helping other women to know God as the father to the fatherless and defender of the widows. The ministry meets every Monday night for a meal provided by the church. While the kids go off to hear Bible lessons and have fun, the moms study the Word and share their stories. The ministry also provides oil changes and home maintenance as needed. Trish knows that God has greater grace over her and her daughter as long as they stay connected to Him and to His church.

When a girl leaves a Mercy home one of our biggest goals is for her to get planted in a healthy local church. Some want to go right back to where they grew up, but in some cases that isn't the best place for them. We challenge girls to get into a church where they will grow spiritually and participate fully as they look to the future.

Being connected to a good church kept me on the right path as a baby Christian. At one time I was one of only a few in my family who walked with God, and I know that lonely feeling of not having supportive people around me. God turned all that around and now my family is very supportive of me and the ministry. But at one time my church was my family. The promise in Psalm 68:6 that God takes the solitary and places them in families was real to me. The church provided the structure and surroundings for my life to grow in Christ.

The Bible is clear about church attendance: "And let us consider how to spur one another to love and to good works. Let us not forsake the assembling of ourselves together, as is the manner of some, but let us exhort one another, especially as you see the Day approaching" (Heb. 10:24–25). Make it a top priority to seek God about what church you should attend, and then get there as quickly as you can and get involved.

STAY IN FELLOWSHIP WITH OTHER BELIEVERS

Being in church is closely related to the next "stay-in": enjoying close fellowship with other believers. Real, life-changing fellowship does not happen automatically. It is possible to go to church every week and even participate in ministry without having real fellowship with the people around you. Some people even have "church friends" and "real friends," two totally separate groups with quite different values.

The Bible tells us we become like what we pay attention to, and what we mostly pay attention to are the people closest to us—family, friends, and workmates. Your goal is to find people who push you toward God, who provoke you to good works, whose lives you want to emulate. The Bible promises that, "Blessed is the man who walks not in the counsel of the ungodly, nor stands in the path of sinners, nor sits in the seat of scoffers" (Ps. 1:1).

Bonnie, a Mercy girl, says that building friendships with believers helped destroy the lie that she was forgotten and unnoticed. God opened her eyes to Zephaniah 3:17, which says that God takes great delight in us. She experienced this through relationships formed at church. She was invited to join a small group and agreed to go, though she did not really know anyone there. She was surprised by the warm, loving welcome she received.

As the Holy Spirit showed her the character of Christ in other people, it fueled her hunger for more of Jesus. She began to love her time alone with Him in the morning, talking to Him, reading His Word, and listening to His Spirit. Because of the relationships around her, Bonnie discovered that Jesus is not against her but for her. She saw His joy, love, and safety in healthy fellowship. Simply attending church was not enough for Bonnie, and it's not enough for you or me. We are built for fellowship. Today Bonnie is living free of the eating disorder that bound her and has a mature relationship with Jesus Christ. She can hardly believe how much she smiles, laughs, and enjoys life. Forming new friendships was a key to her growth.

Allison, who had to overcome her promiscuous past to enjoy her marriage and ministry, says the Christian life started to click for her once she got plugged into a community. For Allison, church gave her a place to put down roots and discover fully who she was in Christ by being open about her past. She overcame her fear of other people knowing what she had done and learned the power of telling her story to people who weren't going to judge her for it. Today she mentors and encourages girls at her church, and is able to use her personal experience to help girls who are brand-new in the Lord and walking through a lot of healing.

Kate, who suddenly found herself a divorced single mother of three girls, made a choice to draw close to specific friends who she knew would encourage her the way God wanted during her divorce. She knew that some of her unsaved friends might rally behind her and urge her to get even. So Kate was careful in those first weeks and months to surround herself with friends who encouraged her to forgive and to go through the divorce amicably, allowing God to really bless her as He promised in Matthew 5:11–12, "Blessed are you when men revile you, and persecute you, and say all kinds of evil against you falsely for My sake. Rejoice and be very glad, because great is your reward in heaven." And then in verse 44, "But I say to you, love your enemies, bless those who curse you, do good to those who hate you, and pray for those who spitefully use you and persecute you" (Matt. 5:44).

This choice also created an environment of peace around Kate. Whatever is going on inside of you affects the environment and the people around you. Some people bring an atmosphere of negativity, fear, insecurity, a critical attitude, and sarcasm into a room. Others bring the presence of God and His joy, peace, patience, kindness, and love. It pays to check the "weather" around your friends. Their conversation and attitude should be setting people free. Hang out with people who add and multiply instead of divide and subtract.

STAY IN ACCOUNTABILITY

Part of fellowship is having accountability with those in your close community. At least some of the people you fellowship with should know potential areas of temptation for you as you overcome them. If they don't know, they can't help. "Iron sharpens iron, so one man sharpens another" (Prov. 27:17, NAS). People can't sharpen you if they don't know what is happening inside you.

Amy, one of our Mercy girls, was molested at age six and spun out into a life of alcohol and drug addiction in an attempt to mask the torment of those memories. She stole from her family members and others to feed the addiction and get money for her lifestyle. In time she found herself living in one of the worst ghettos in her town and doing anything to survive and stay high, including prostitution. A suicide attempt put her into a coma for several days. When she awoke, the first coherent words she heard came from the Lord. He said, "I have plans to prosper you."

Amy had never read the Bible, but an extended family member printed the Mercy application for her. God worked powerfully in Amy's life at Mercy, and when she graduated from our program she chose to surround herself with strong Christians she could learn from. She continued to grow. Amy tenaciously held on to the freedom she found in Christ and would not let go, which is why today she is totally free of past bondages.

Even if there are no life-controlling issues in your past, everyone should have an accountability person or two in his life. For example, one of my friends is single and in her thirties. Every time she goes on a date she tells a friend beforehand, "I'm going on a date. I need you to call me in the middle of it to check on me." Does she intend to fall into sin? No, but she is intentional about accountability. She puts safeguards in her life.

Some people can establish an accountability relationship with friends they already have. Some might want to start an accountability relationship with someone in your small group. Look for a mature Christian who is not intimidated easily, and is willing to be honest, to pray, and to call you to account if necessary. Starting that relationship comes down to telling someone you trust, "I'd like someone to hold me accountable with this weakness or struggle I'm having. Are you willing to be that person?"

The best steps then are to establish an expectation for communication and interaction. How often will you check in? Does the accountable person have permission to call or text when struggling? Will you meet regularly and talk about how things are going? The time you spend with your accountability partner should be strategic and intentional. In some cases you will want to have goals you are working toward until the next time you meet. Remember not to place too great of a burden on the accountability partner. His or her role is to be a supportive cheerleader, not a counselor or caretaker.

One former resident who struggled with an eating disorder says having accountability with friends was an important reason she did not go back to the eating disorder. When she was tempted to go back to eating disorder behaviors, she would call someone to actually sit with her while she ate. Talk about intentional freedom! I'm so proud of her.

Lesli, who also overcame an eating disorder, guards against her weakness by not isolating herself from others. She has godly friends and stays connected to church and small groups. She also has accountability partners. Knowing that she has to give an account for her actions makes her think twice when tempted to give in to her struggle. As a result, God has taken her eight-year battle with an eating disorder and turned it into greater dependence upon Him. Her greatest trials, she says, have produced the most intimate times she has had with the Lord.

We hear testimonies like this all the time, and, truthfully, accountability should be a big part of all of our lives. The reality is that every leader should be accountable, regardless of the size of the company, business, ministry, or church that he or she may lead. Accountability is a lifestyle for all of us, not just a season. The partner may change over time, but the purpose remains to stay free in Christ.

On a side note, if you are the smartest, most spiritual person in your group of friends, you may want to consider enlarging your group. We all need people in our lives who will challenge us whenever it is needed, and we all need it at different times and seasons of our lives. Make the right friends because those friends will make you.

Establish Safe Routines

Accountability also means creating a safe lifestyle for yourself. As kids, my siblings and I were members of the 4H club. My dad owned Black Angus cattle, and we would show them in the county fair. Each of us had to learn how to comb them down, give them a bath, put their holsters on and off, and walk them around the ring so the judges could make their decision. As tedious as it was sometimes, I liked the routine of grooming and showing the cattle.

The routine I didn't like was helping Mom with the vegetables in our garden. We had to shuck corn, snap beans, and help her can and freeze what we grew, not to mention constantly pull weeds from the garden.

Those things taught me a lesson: good routines lead to good results. They keep you out of trouble. They give your life healthy boundaries. They set you up to win.

At Mercy we know that safety is established through good structures and routines. In other residential recovery programs a lot of the activities are optional. At Mercy, nothing is optional. Residents must fully participate in everything. The entire schedule is intentional and planned. Residents don't get to wade in—they jump in from day one.

I encourage you to have that same attitude toward your freedom by creating the right routines. All habits, good and bad, are ritualistic by nature. Your job is to create healthy routines to replace unhealthy ones. Tell yourself when you are going to wake up and decide in advance the very first thing you will do. I encourage you to start by thanking the Lord and reading something from the Bible. Then go through your day with predictable, preplanned routines in each area. If you are tempted by something, create routines that avoid it or strengthen you against it. You might avoid certain places or people. You might set limits for

Internet usage or coffee consumption or conversations of a certain nature. Whatever it is, make the routine intentional and stick to your commitment.

Emily, a Mercy girl, recognized that lying, silence, and deception had been major strongholds of the enemy in her life and that the only way to break their power was through rigorous honesty. She knew she was only as accountable as she chose to be. A verse that spoke strongly to her was Psalm 32:3–5:

> When I refused to confess my sin, my body wasted away, and I groaned all day long. Day and night your hand of discipline was heavy on me. My strength evaporated like water in the summer heat. Finally, I confessed all my sins to you and stopped trying to hide my guilt. I said to myself, "I will confess my rebellion to the LORD." And you forgave me! All my guilt is gone.
>
> —NLT

Emily struggled with eating disorders, and to work against those temptations she created a routine where she ate at a certain time and, when possible, with other people. She did not allow herself to go to the bathroom right after a meal. She limited her exercise to a certain level and found people to hold her accountable to those limits. She even checked her own motive when working out and asked herself, "Am I doing it because it is healthy and I want to, or am I doing it because I feel like I have to?"

Today, Emily is pursuing a doctorate of veterinary medicine. One day she hopes to work with other young girls who have gone through similar struggles. Emily says her daily purpose is summed up in Philippians 3:10, "[For my determined purpose is] that I may know Him" (AMP).

Like Emily and many others, be intentional about your schedule. Don't just cast yourself to the winds and hope everything works out OK. Get on your calendar and decide now, rather than in the moment, what you will do, where you will go, and how you will live. You won't get it perfect all the time, but it will put guard rails on your life and spare you much pain and bondage.

Breaking Soul Ties

> Even though I hated him, I always felt drawn toward him and didn't know why. I didn't realize then that my soul had been violated along with my body. Once I prayed and broke that tie, I felt so free and unattached from my abuser. God really is putting me back together again in my mind, body, and soul.
>
> —"Martha"

Sometimes choosing the right friends and routines means making a very deliberate break with old friends and old routines. Some relationships grow so close that your soul feels strongly attached to another person or habit. We call this a soul tie, the knitting together of two people at a strong level. In the right context, such as marriage, the knitting of two souls brings tremendous blessing. Outside of marriage or in the wrong context it can bring tremendous destruction. This unhealthy connection affects everything from your mood to the decisions you make to how you relate to God. It usually brings ongoing confusion and unhealthy feelings of attachment.

Soul ties are not always sexual. A woman I'll call Ellie used to talk with her mother every day, but realized that her mother was becoming a negative influence on her with her guilt trips, emotional manipulation, and bad attitude. Those phone calls took their toll until one day Ellie decided to stop talking to her mom so frequently. She felt that her mom needed to cultivate stronger friendships with other people and stop depending on her so much.

Ellie had a tough conversation with her mom and told her she was limiting their phone calls to one a week in hopes that her mom would build friendships with others, decide to have healthier emotions, and choose better ways of relating. As you can imagine, her mom was mad, but Ellie stood strong and wouldn't be drawn into argument or emotional manipulation. Ellie recruited some friends to give her accountability about not talking with her mom more than she should. After a while Ellie's mom did reach out to other people, and a couple of years later she and Ellie were talking almost daily again but in a much healthier way. Ellie actually wanted to talk, and her mom was much more positive and encouraging. It took work setting and keeping boundaries, but the result was worth it.

If you feel strongly tied to someone in an unhealthy way, you need to redefine that relationship. It may mean cutting it off entirely if it has been sinful and destructive. Or it may mean redefining it as Ellie did, setting new boundaries and creating a better emotional atmosphere. If you would like to make that break, I encourage you to pray, "Lord, I choose to break this unhealthy relationship and choose to have healthy relationships in my life. I renounce that old relationship and any attachment I have to it, in Jesus's name. It no longer has power over me." You might write names on a white board and erase them to symbolize the change you are making. The point is to free your soul of ungodly ties and fully commit your relationships to Christ. He will complete the work of cleansing you from unhealthy attachments.

The steps and advice in this chapter are hard-won. In thirty-plus years of ministry we find that when girls fall off the map after leaving Mercy, it's almost always because they stop doing one or more of these things. By God's grace most of our graduates stick to these "stay-ins" and set a course for freedom in their lives.

How about you? Are you willing to make the necessary changes at the daily level to sustain your freedom? Are you willing to set yourself up for lifelong success? I often think of the girls who come to us at Mercy. They take a huge step into the unknown when they arrive at one of our homes. They walk away from their old lives. They give up six months to follow a bunch of rules they never had to follow before. It's confusing and uncomfortable for them sometimes. It takes real commitment to choose that new direction and say good-bye to old, familiar things.

Are you willing to make that commitment to stay in freedom? If so, God will help you all the way. Does this mean you should expect perfection from yourself? Of course not. When a baby learns to walk, his parents do not scold him when he falls. They are excited to see him learning and growing. God looks at you with great joy as you do your best to walk in Him. When you fall, He smiles, picks you up, and sends you on your way to try again. The key is to be faithful and relentlessly come back to the path of freedom. Remember, the Bible says, "For a righteous man may fall seven times and rise again" (Prov. 24:16, NKJV).

Now we will look to your future—the grand vision God has for your life, which is one of the reasons He wants you free.

Chapter 8

UNLOCKING YOUR FUTURE

A FTER WE OPENED our first Mercy home in Monroe, Louisiana, God was leading us to build a second home, this one to be located in Nashville. I was excited about our growing future but had no idea where exactly to build the home. As I was in prayer one day about it, God showed me an image of hills and trees. I knew then that we were supposed to be on a piece of property with hills and trees. Thinking it would be located in the countryside, I went for a drive and looked for properties for sale with hills and trees like the ones I had seen. Every time I found such a property and took it to the zoning board, they denied my request to build a girls' residential home there. After about five times presenting properties to the zoning board and having my requests denied I said to them, "You're turning down everything I bring to you, so I may as well ask: what will you zone?"

They said, "We will zone property in a commercial area. It doesn't have to be commercial property, but it has to be in a commercial area."

I went out looking with our real estate agent, a good guy who went to church with me, and told him what the board had said. "I don't think there's a commercial property with hills and trees on it in all of Nashville," he said. I assured him, "There's got to be, 'cause I saw it." So we pulled over to the side of the road and prayed, asking God to show us exactly where the property was, and left it at that. That was a Friday afternoon.

On Monday morning the agent called me: "I found your hills and trees," he said.

"You did?" I replied.

He started laughing. There was five acres with hills and a thick row of trees right next door to the church we both attended. That was the beginning of our Mercy home and headquarters in Nashville. It turned out to be the perfect location. Of course, God knew that.

Before anything was built on that property, I would drive onto it regularly to pray and thank God in advance for what He was going to do. God had shown us there would be two buildings, one a headquarters and the other a home. I saw them in my spirit before they happened in the natural. I knew the vision that He had given to me so I thanked God in advance for the buildings being built debt-free and for the lives that would be transformed. I dedicated the buildings to the work of God and declared that thousands of lives would be changed for His glory, hundreds of babies would be saved from abortion, and on and on. It took five years to come to pass, and when it did the reality was bigger and better than even what I had spoken and thanked Him for.

God had given me a vision for the future and I believed it, spoke it, and lived it until it became a present reality. Having a vision for our future means not living in the story of our past. It means looking ahead with hope and faith in the good things God will do. Too much conventional wisdom and secular counseling makes our problems the center focus. At Mercy we are convinced that vision and hope for the future are pivotal to the healing process. It's one of the reasons we start Aftercare Planning halfway through the process—because the future is bigger than our past and deserves a lot more attention.

Having vision and hope for the future actually helps us deal with tough things in the present. We shouldn't delay looking to the future until we "solve" what is in our pasts. Instead we should look to the future while dealing with the difficult things so that we get the right perspective and put the past in its proper place.

I am convinced God has a vision for you and your future. How will you recognize it? A godly vision has the following characteristics:

1. It is big. By "big" I don't mean always big in numbers or size. I mean big in your heart, big in purpose, big in its meaning to God. It's more than you and your resources and ability can accomplish. If you can do it by yourself, then you don't need God, and that kind of vision would not be from Him. It will challenge and change your heart.

This does not mean your vision has to be about starting a ministry. It might be much "smaller" by outward appearances, or more personal. Your vision might be to have healthy relationships with your coworkers, or to serve your boss well, or to establish new patterns of communication in your family or marriage. It might be to get a different job, establish a consistent prayer life, or be less critical. God can give us vision for every area of our lives if we ask Him. Some will seem small and some will seem outrageously big—and they are all important to God.

2. It is exciting. God created us for adventure and risk. If we don't find excitement in God's plan, we will hunt for excitement elsewhere. The vision God has for you will be thrilling and heart-stopping at times. Get on board and hold on.

3. It is real. The vision God gave me of the Nashville property was visual—I saw hills and trees clearly in my mind. Other visions are of the heart; we know them to be true before there is any evidence. Some people consider visions and seeing things in our minds to be weird and imaginary, but the truth is there is nothing more real than a God-given vision. Hebrews 11:1 tells us that "faith is the substance of things hoped for, the evidence of things not seen." The vision is real in the heart of God, and you can often see it with the eyes of your spirit. Even though I could not physically see the hills and trees, I could picture them in my mind and see the vision with the eyes of my heart.

4. It directs and defines your life. Vision is not optional in the Christian journey. To walk in freedom for very long, we must have a vision for our future that is specific to us and our purpose on earth. Otherwise we will wander and stray. Vision gives us focus, direction, and purpose. It gives us a desire to get rid of everything that distracts us. Proverbs 3:5–6 says, "Trust in the LORD with all your heart, and lean not on your own understanding; in all your ways acknowledge Him, and He will direct your paths." Habakkuk 2:2 also says to write the vision. In the old days, they wrote it on tablets of stone. Today at Mercy, we make a DVD so that everyone can see the vision with their own eyes.

Some girls at our homes get stuck talking about their baggage. One of the best ways we have found to free them from backward thinking is to get them to dream about their future. We remind them that Jeremiah 29:11 says, "'For I know the plans I have for you,' declares the LORD, 'plans to prosper you and not to harm you, plans to give you hope and a future'" (NIV). We also remind them that 2 Corinthians 5:17 says that if you are a new creation in Christ, old things have passed away and all things are new.

I remember years ago when one of our counselors was meeting with a girl and had to remind her of this very thing—that God's plans and purposes for her and her future were for good, and it was not going to be a repeat of past pain and abuse that she had experienced. At that point, this young woman finally started developing a vision for her life. She graduated, got married, and recently earned her master's degree. Would that have happened had she kept magnifying the problem and identifying with her past? I don't think so.

What is God leading you to do? Could you write down the vision for your life right now? Have you ever caught a glimpse of it? Has God revealed it to you in prayer? Sometimes at Mercy we encourage girls to reconnect with the hopes and dreams they had before things took a wrong turn in their lives—before the pain warped everything. It may be time for you to reconnect with a vision that was lost many years ago. God said in Jeremiah 1:5, "Before I formed you in the womb I knew you, before you were born I set you apart; I appointed you as a prophet to the nations" (NIV). God had a big vision for Jeremiah before Jeremiah was even conceived!

I believe the same is true of every person. The destiny God has for you is greater than you can imagine. God said later through Jeremiah, "'Then you will call on me and come and pray to me, and I will listen to you. You will seek me and find me when you seek me with all your heart. I will be found by you,' declares the LORD" (Jer. 29:12–14, NIV). After all, it says in Hebrews 11:6 that God is a rewarder of those who diligently seek Him. That is the perfect prescription for finding our vision. We must passionately pursue it, seeking Him with all our hearts.

VISION BUILDING

A great way to seek Him and enlarge your vision is by looking at what God has done in other people's lives. As a young woman I inundated myself with books by George Müller, Corrie ten Boom, David Wilkerson, Nicky Cruz, Cookie Rodriguez—everything I could get my hands on that had to do with people whose lives have been transformed: orphans, addicts, gang members, and people coming out of prison. I became as obsessed with those books as I was with sports biographies when I was a kid. I am drawn to pioneers of life-giving and life-transformation organizations. Their faith experiences helped build the vision for my future.

One of the best visions for my life came from a female pastor in Monroe, Louisiana. Lea Joyner, who was older than me by a few decades and never married, was arguably the most influential minister in the city. The mayor often asked her to lead prayers at prayer breakfasts and public events. In her particular denomination, pastors were often moved around to another church every few years. However, at Lea's request, she was given a small church with a handful of people and was allowed to stay with it for a long time. She built it into a large church filled with a growing community of believers in Monroe. She was a precious and sweet woman with big faith and a huge influence in her city.

Lea was very encouraging to me when I moved to West Monroe to start the first Mercy home. She found out about me through the newspaper and saw me as someone like her, who had vision and a heart to make a difference. She showed me around her church and took time on numerous occasions to share her wisdom with me. I particularly remember photos on the wall depicting the growth of the church under her leadership. It had started in a tiny building and eventually grew to the size of a whole city block with an array of ministries to the homeless and outcast.

Lea had a huge impact on my life and I was in awe of her. She demonstrated that if your heart is truly about helping people then God will draw the hurting to you. Her example taught me to have authentic love for people and not to quit. I had the privilege of speaking at her church several times. She would send me notes saying, "I'm praying for you. Keep on keeping on." She would share scriptures with me that had encouraged her. She taught me that if you were faithful in little, God will give you much.

It was a daily routine for Lea's assistant to call and wake her every morning at 4:45 a.m. to begin her day. I remember getting a call from her assistant fairly early one morning asking if I had heard from Lea. She knew that Lea occasionally checked in with me to encourage me and see how I was doing in my journey with Mercy. For the first time in years, Lea had not answered her wake-up call that morning. Her secretary told me that she had gone to Lea's home, but Lea was not there. She had then driven over to the church, where she found Lea's broken eyeglasses and drops of blood in the parking lot. She quickly reported this to the police.

My heart sank at this news, because I knew something had gone horribly wrong and this was a potentially serious situation. Plans were made that day by the entire community for a huge citywide prayer service for Lea, and all the news stations covered the story because of her stature in the city. Prayer went on for two straight days until they found Lea's stolen car in Arkansas and her body dumped out near the Ouachita River. Lea had been raped and brutally beaten by someone to whom she had reached out to bring hope and healing.

When Lea died, the city named a prominent bridge after her, and the church renamed itself Lea Joyner Methodist Church. It was the biggest funeral I have ever seen for one of the greatest women I have ever known—so large that it took place at the Monroe Convention Center with thousands in attendance, including the entire Monroe Police Department.

Lea was a stranger to me until I moved to West Monroe, but she did so much to put a vision in my heart for what Mercy could become. That was in stark contrast to what some of my own friends back home did. When I was ready to launch Mercy, I sought wisdom from a family who had become like my family away from home. They had done a lot to encourage me in my faith. So it was with great expectation that I went to seek their encouragement and wisdom about starting Mercy. I was shocked by their response.

"There is no way that will work," they said after I shared my vision with them.

I was floored. It was true that I had no money, yet here I was declaring I was going to open a home and staff it professionally, pay counselors the same as if they worked in a secular setting, create a first-class program, and tithe as a ministry so we wouldn't have a poverty mentality. Not only that but I would refuse to take government money and would accept the girls who wanted help free of charge. None of that made sense to the natural mind. But that was the point. If it had made any sense, anyone could have done it. When you have a God-given, impossible dream, that's when it gets fun. Once again, if it can be done by humans, why do we need God? We are called to step into the unknown, put things on the line, be risk takers, and decide if we really believe what God said.

Still, I was devastated at their response. I wanted to hear, "That is so awesome, Nancy! Go for it!" I learned then that you have to be careful with whom you share your dreams. Some people may encourage you to stay in your comfort zone, but Hebrews 11:6 says that without faith, it is impossible to please God. Faith requires that we step beyond our comfort zone, and as we step out in obedience, God will step out with us.

A Vision Keeps You on Track

When a girl walks through the door of a Mercy home looking rough and hopeless, our vision is sustained by what God has done in the lives of other girls who have walked through our doors since 1983 and graduated from our program. Given the miracles we have seen Him do in so many girls over the years, it's not that difficult to believe he will do it again. God says, "I am the Lord thy God. I change not. I will not alter the thing that came from my mouth." (See Malachi 3:6 and Psalm 89:34). We know that He came to heal the brokenhearted and set the captives free (Isa. 61). Our faith is strong even when transformation seems slow because the Bible teaches that Jesus Christ is the same yesterday, today, and forever (Heb. 13:8). If He changed someone yesterday, He'll do it today and tomorrow as well. His Word does not return void (Isa. 55:11). So like Paul told Timothy, we stir up that vision in us (2 Tim. 1:6). We find the boldness to declare that every spiritual captive who walks into Mercy will be set free to walk in total freedom. Period.

Even when a girl is not moving ahead very quickly we don't get into the habit of saying, "This girl is stuck. She's not making any progress." Instead we boldly speak the good things and minimize the negative. We keep the atmosphere of faith with our words and our attitudes. We relentlessly hold to the vision that each girl has a future and that her past will not destroy her future.

Stick with the vision God gives you, not being distracted by the apparent slowness or failure around you. Proverbs 4:25–27 says, "Let your eyes look straight ahead; fix your gaze directly before you. Give careful thought to the paths for your feet and be steadfast in all your ways. Do not turn to the right or the left; keep your foot from evil" (NIV). That is great, practical advice for the long haul.

IN HIS TIME

When God gives a vision we must also be mindful of His timing. It's not as simple as rushing out and doing it in our own strength. In our excitement and passion sometimes it is easy to get ahead of His pace.

I found that out for myself in the very beginning of my ministry. When we started, a real estate agent who loved the vision for Mercy donated an office building on a main street in Monroe, and we worked out of that office. He believed that we would one day have a residential home but knew that we needed a place to start.

As I would go out and speak in the community at youth events, churches, and civic groups we began to receive calls from young women who were desperate for help and who had all kinds of issues. They came to us from college campuses, flop houses, and the streets. Some still lived with their parents. We tried to help as much as we could through counseling and encouragement, but I began to feel the pressure to open a home, and I grew impatient.

There was one particular girl who had great potential but was struggling with a very serious drug addiction. She had been coming in to see us for counseling, but on this particular day she did not show up for her appointment. I called one of my friends who was a prayer partner and who knew this young woman and where she lived. We met and went over to her house to check on her. We could see through the window that she was lying unconscious on the floor. We found a window that was unlatched and called the ambulance. They arrived quickly and transferred her to the hospital, where her stomach was pumped. She nearly died from an overdose, but thankfully they were able to pull her through.

"This girl almost died," I thought afterward. "We have to get a residential home going."

Moved by the needs of girls like her, I yielded to my desire to move quickly instead of being led by the Spirit. Rather than take the necessary steps to lay a strong foundation, both financially and in staff training and experience, I jumped ahead of God's timing. I didn't pray or ask God; I just went out, leased a house, and filled it with eight girls who needed help. I now realize that I was driven by the need rather than being led by the Spirit.

Immediately, the faucet of finances that had been flowing stopped. It was like someone had turned a knob—it was that sudden. Donors who had been giving faithfully stopped giving. I began to realize I had made a mistake. I had no peace about opening the house. I had acted out of a sense of urgency.

"What am I going to do?" I asked God in a time of soul-searching. "What did I do wrong?"

I felt Him impress upon my heart, "I didn't lead you to open that home. You did it all by yourself. You can either back up and admit you made a mistake and wait on My timing, or you can press ahead, yet this ministry will never be fully what it should be. I can bless your mistake to a point if you want to continue on, but if you want the bigger blessing and the real vision I have for you, then you have to shut the house down and back up."

By this time front page newspaper headlines blared that we were shutting down due to lack of funds. I had false-started like someone jumping the gun at a track meet. I'm a bit of a bulldozer and hate giving up ground that I have taken, but I wanted the bigger blessing and there was only one way to get it. I had to admit I was wrong. I went in front of the staff, told them I was wrong, that I had gotten ahead of God's timing and that I was going to close the residential home until God clearly revealed His timing.

Peace came immediately. Everyone was in agreement that it was the right thing to do. Money started flowing in again along with new speaking invitations. We could feel God's blessing on our decision to step back and get in His timing.

Getting a vision is one thing, but timing is so critical. Habakkuk 2:3 says though the vision tarry, wait for it. It will surely come. Sometimes the best thing we can do for our vision is to wait for it in faith and patience (Heb. 6:12).

That situation humbled me, but it also gave me great confidence. People came up to me in the grocery store and said, "We're so sorry that home didn't work out for you." I said with full assurance, "Oh, it'll definitely work out. I just got ahead of myself." And I was right, because I was back on God's schedule.

A few weeks later I stopped at a convenience store to fill up my car with gas. As I was pulling out of the parking lot, I clearly heard in my heart, "Go get a newspaper." I turned around and pulled into a parking spot, went inside, and bought the newspaper. Instead of turning straight to the sports page like I usually do, I flipped to the classifieds. There I looked at every piece of property for sale. The last listing in those classifieds described a home for sale, which became our first Mercy home. Something jumped in my heart that this was from God, but I wanted to seek confirmation from my board of directors. We immediately made an appointment with the real estate agent for a couple of board members and me to go and look at the property. We eventually brought the rest of the board over, and after much prayer we all agreed that this was the right place and the right time.

Let God develop your vision at His pace, even if it is slower than what you would like. Go for the bigger blessing, the full vision. My dream now is to break ground on our home in Florida. As of this writing it is a bare piece of property, just like the Nashville property was at one time. Every time I go to north Florida I walk on that property and pray for the house to come up out of the ground debt-free, thanking God in advance for what He is going to do, just like I did in Nashville. A local church there sends prayer teams to walk over that property, too, making faith declarations over it that the vision will come to pass. In God's timing, I know it will happen.

GIVING TO YOUR VISION

The other thing you can do to accomplish your vision is to sow into someone else's God-given vision today. This is an important step that so many people miss. The basic principle for increase in your life is found in the first chapter of the Bible where it says the "seed is in itself" (Gen. 1:11, NKJV). That means the seed for what you need is in what you sow. If you need love, sow love. If you need friends, sow friendliness (Prov. 18:24). If you need money, sow money. "Give, and it will be given to you: Good measure, pressed down, shaken together, and running over will men give unto you. For with the measure you use, it will be measured unto you" (Luke 6:38).

I grew up on a farm and sowing was a normal part of life for me. I would see my dad sow crops every year so we had something to feed the cow and to eat for dinner. Sowing was a very practical reality. When I met the Lord I started sowing into His work right away. Sometimes I would write a tithe check even though my bank account said I didn't have enough to live on that month. It didn't matter to me—it was the first check I wrote every month. It was always amazing to me how, even though on paper it didn't look like it, I always had more than enough money each month when I was faithful to write that tithe check.

I knew I would never reap if I didn't sow. Reaping didn't always come quickly or in the way I thought, but it always happened. Our job is simply to be consistent in sowing. It will always come back to bless us in whatever form God decides.

This happened to me in college in an unexpected way. I was working forty hours a week and going to school full time, so I was busy. But I was very diligent at work and went above and beyond for my employer. God blesses diligence. Being faithful and diligent at work is a way of sowing into someone else's vision. God will open doors of promotion for you as He did for me. I was blessed with an offer of a full-time position. Now they were paying me as if I had graduated from college while I was still finishing my degree. The schedule was intense: I went to school in the mornings in Murfreesboro from eight to noon, drove an hour to work, worked a full day, then drove an hour home. There were times I had to roll the window down so the cold air would keep me awake. I didn't sleep much.

A few months into that schedule, the Department of Corrections let me know that anyone working in their field of study while attending university could receive a full scholarship to enable them to finish school. It meant that I didn't have to pay any more tuition. It was paid for by the State of Tennessee because I was earning a degree in criminal justice while working for the Department of Corrections. I knew right away, "This is God blessing me because I'm tithing and being diligent at work." I knew I was reaping what I had sown. I have proven the sowing and reaping principle from the Bible a thousand times since then.

Scripture says, "Be not deceived. God is not mocked. For whatever a man sows, that will he also reap" (Gal. 6:7). I see that as a great promise because I know that if I'm giving, God will cause me to reap abundantly. It is one of the most hopeful passages in all the Bible. It goes on to say, "And let us not grow weary in doing good, for in due season we shall reap, if we do not give up" (Gal. 6:9). People often say, "What goes around comes around." They mean it negatively, but I like to say it positively. What you do and give and say will come back to you.

You may wonder why we're talking about tithing and financial giving in a book about ditching your baggage. The truth is that if you give, God will rebuke the devourer for your sake and open up the windows of heaven, as it says in Malachi 3:11. If we are not obedient in giving, it leaves an open door for the enemy to steal from us. So giving to God in tithes and offerings is not only an act of worship, it is an act of warfare. It opens the doors for God to send unexpected blessings our way because of our obedience.

Giving also means giving of our energy and time. When we volunteer for some good work or commit to help others in an area where they need help, God will use that to heal us. At Mercy we have had people volunteer to work with us who were going through their own struggles with family or children. Their giving became an important part of their own healing process. Giving of our time and talents as well as treasure will enlarge our vision, get our eyes off ourselves, and put us in an atmosphere where God can teach, heal, and inspire us.

I encourage you to stretch yourself in giving. Help other people reach their goals and expand their visions. As you do, God will supernaturally supply for your vision, as He has so faithfully with Mercy.

Sow with expectation.

Sow with consistency.

Sow in good soil.

You will reap in due time!

As you are sowing, cultivate vision in your own heart. Direct your thoughts more to the future than to the past. Be constant in hope, as the Bible says. Hope is not just a good idea or a nice thought; it is the only acceptable attitude of the heart for a person walking in freedom. Let hope inspire vision for positive change and transformation in your life. Do these things to cultivate it:

1. Write the vision. Make it plain so you and others can read it. Don't let it become blurry or vague in your memory. Write it down and keep it at the forefront of your mind.

2. Speak the vision. I've proven this time and again. Let the vision come out of your mouth. God spoke creation into existence, and we are wise to follow His example. Speak your vision out loud.

3. Pray the vision. The psalms and books written by the prophets (Jeremiah, Isaiah, Ezekiel, Joshua, etc.) are

full of examples of reminding God of His promises. Of course, God never forgets. By praying the vision back to Him we are reminding ourselves of His faithfulness and locking into agreement with God.

4. Wait on the vision. Don't rush like I did and find yourself ahead of God's timing.

5. Give to other visions. Sow generously of your time, talent, and treasure. However big you want your vision to be, that should determine the measure of your giving.

I'm excited about how God will fulfill your vision! I am excited for your future because I know that God has great things ahead of you.

CONCLUSION

Freedom is yours! Let's take a moment to look at some of the important principles and life-transforming truths we have talked about in this book:

❀ Transformation takes total commitment. We can't treat Jesus like a part-time lover or pick and choose what to believe like we're in a buffet line and expect to walk in total freedom.

❀ God is not waiting for us to get our stuff together before coming to Him for help. He wants us now, whatever baggage we have.

❀ Life-controlling problems are not forever. It's a lie of the enemy that you will never get free or that you will always be a "recovering" whatever. Throw that idea away.

❀ Forgiveness is a big part of living in freedom. Forgiveness almost never feels natural or comfortable at first. It is a choice, not a feeling, but your feelings will follow when you make the sincere commitment to forgive.

❀ God is never bad, and Satan, the enemy of our souls, is never good. This one principle can change your view of God and literally transform your life all by itself.

❀ Revenge belongs to God. He can do a lot better job than we can, and He does it with perfect justice and mercy. We can trust Him to right every wrong we have experienced.

❀ Getting God's perspective on our lives means replacing untrue thoughts with truth from God's Word.

❀ Choosing the right friends helps us maintain God's perspective on our situations.

❀ Reading and meditating on God's Word is critical. I encourage everyone to *summarize, personalize,* and *vocalize* the scriptures they read, which will give us great power in our lives and circumstances.

❀ Getting God's perspective by renewing our minds is an active, ongoing process that leads to greater freedom as we toss out lies and build our lives on Christ, the solid foundation.

❀ Breaking family patterns helps us to break habits that have kept generations bound. We break family patterns by identifying them and taking authority over them based on our authority as followers of Jesus.

❀ Healing life's hurts means acknowledging them and inviting God's perspective on what happened. We all need healing because we all get hurt, and allowing God to heal our hurts brings a great deal of freedom and peace.

❀ God has given us power to overcome oppression in our lives. It starts by submitting to God and closing the door on choices that result in loss of freedom. Having experienced freedom from the oppression of a life-controlling eating disorder, I know you can choose freedom from whatever is oppressing you!

❀ Walking in freedom for a lifetime means staying in prayer, staying in the Word, staying in church, and staying in fellowship and accountability with other strong believers.

❀ God's vision for your future will be hope-filled and exciting. Focusing on and moving toward that vision will energize your life and keep you on the path of freedom.

I am so excited about what's next. Jesus has won the victory and given you the power to walk in life and peace. I hope that these principles have powerfully connected you to God's plan for your life and will bring lasting life change not just this week, this month, and this year but for the rest of your days. I am confident that God has made this book a turning point in the lives of many people. They have chosen to ditch the baggage and choose life, as the Bible so powerfully says:

> Today I have given you the choice between life and death, between blessings and curses. Now I call on heaven and earth to witness the choice you make. Oh, that you would choose life, so that you and your descendants might live!
> —DEUTERONOMY 30:19, NLT

I am proud of you for setting your heart and mind to choose blessings and life. God has built you for success, not failure. In

Him each one of us is called to greatness. Whatever held you back before is gone. We give it no honor. Rather,

> We all, with unveiled face, beholding the glory of the Lord, are being transformed into the same image from one degree of glory to another. For this comes from the Lord who is the Spirit.
>
> —2 Corinthians 3:18, esv

I'm excited about the life of victory that is ahead of you, and not just for you but for your children, your grandchildren, your nieces and nephews, and anyone else you influence. Your victory is designed to grow and impact everyone around you. You are becoming a shining example of God's grace in the midst of whatever situation you are in. If you stumble, shake the dust off and get right back on the road of freedom. I love the words of the prophet Isaiah:

> Awake, awake! Put on your strength, O Zion; put on your beautiful garments...Shake yourself from the dust; arise...Loose yourself from the bonds of your neck, O captive daughter of Zion.
>
> —Isaiah 52:1–2

That old baggage doesn't belong to you anymore. Everything you need is where you are going. You are free!

We would love to hear your testimonies of how God is using the teaching in this book to help you along your journey. Feel free to e-mail or write to us so we can rejoice with you and partner with you in prayer.

I firmly believe in the keys and principles outlined in this book because I have seen them work time and time again. At Mercy, we plan to expand our reach and help others outside the walls of Mercy realize this kind of lasting freedom. We are going to multiply our efforts and watch God multiply His freedom. Visit www.MercyMultiplied.com for more resources and to see how you can get involved in helping others ditch their baggage and change their lives!

IN FREEDOM,

NANCY ALCORN

APPENDIX

Practice saying these verses out loud to help renew your mind with God's Word.

- ❀ I am a child of God. "To all who believed him and accepted him, he gave the right to become children of God" (John 1:12, NLT).

- ❀ I am the light of the world. "You are the light of the world—like a city on a hilltop that cannot be hidden" (Matt. 5:14, NLT).

- ❀ I am a joint heir with Christ. "Since we are his children, we are his heirs. In fact, together with Christ we are heirs of God's glory" (Rom. 8:17, NLT).

- ❀ I am a temple, a dwelling place of God. "Don't you realize that your body is the temple of the Holy Spirit, who lives in you and was given to you by God?" (1 Cor. 6:19, NLT).

- ❀ I am a new creation. "Anyone who belongs to Christ has become a new person. The old life is gone; a new life has begun!" (2 Cor. 5:17, NLT).

- ❀ I am righteous and holy. "Put on your new nature, created to be like God—truly righteous and holy" (Eph. 4:24, NLT).

❋ I am a threat to the devil. "I have given you authority to trample on snakes and scorpions and to overcome all the power of the enemy; nothing will harm you" (Luke 10:19, NIV).

❋ I am free from condemnation. "There is no condemnation for those who belong to Christ Jesus" (Rom. 8:1, NLT).

❋ I may approach God with confidence. "Because of Christ and our faith in him, we can now come boldly and confidently into God's presence" (Eph. 3:12, NLT).

❋ I am complete in Christ. "You also are complete through your union with Christ, who is the head over every ruler and authority" (Col. 2:10, NLT).

❋ I have been redeemed and forgiven from all of my sins. "He has rescued us from the kingdom of darkness and transferred us into the Kingdom of his dear Son, who purchased our freedom and forgave our sins" (Col. 1:13–14, NLT).

❋ I am of the light and no longer belong to the darkness. "You are all children of the light and children of the day. We do not belong to the night or to the darkness" (1 Thess. 5:5, NIV).

❋ I am chosen. "For you are a people holy to the LORD your God. The LORD your God has chosen you out of all the peoples on the face of the earth to be his people, his treasured possession" (Deut. 7:6, NIV).

❋ I am beautiful and flawless. "You are altogether beautiful, my darling; there is no flaw in you" (Song of Sol. 4:7, NIV).

❀ I have peace. "The LORD gives strength to his people; the LORD blesses his people with peace" (Ps. 29:11, NIV).

❀ I am accepted. "Accept one another, then, just as Christ accepted you, in order to bring praise to God" (Rom. 15:7, NIV).

❀ I am a more than a conqueror. "In all these things we are more than conquerors through him who loved us" (Rom. 8:37, NIV).

❀ I am confident and fearless. "For God has not given us a spirit of fear and timidity, but of power, love, and self-discipline" (2 Tim. 1:7, NLT).

❀ I am treasured. "For you are a people holy to the LORD your God. The LORD your God has chosen you out of all the peoples on the face of the earth to be his people, his treasured possession" (Deut. 7:6, NIV).

❀ I am worthy of His love. "They will walk with me, dressed in white, for they are worthy" (Rev. 3:4, NIV).

❀ I am a delight to God. "For the LORD takes delight in his people" (Ps. 149:4, NIV).

❀ I am secure. "Let the beloved of the LORD rest secure in him, for he shields him all day long, and the one the LORD loves rests between his shoulders" (Deut. 33:12, NIV).

❀ I am loved unconditionally. "Neither height nor depth, nor anything else in all creation, will be able to separate us from the love of God that is in Christ Jesus our Lord" (Rom. 8:39, NIV).

❀ I am gifted. "We have different gifts, according to the grace given to each of us" (Rom. 12:6, NIV).

❀ I am created in the image of God. "God created human beings in his own image" (Gen. 1:27, NLT).

❀ I am a citizen of heaven. "But we are citizens of heaven, where the Lord Jesus Christ lives. And we are eagerly waiting for him to return as our Savior" (Phil. 3:20, NLT).

DITCH THE BAGGAGE

If you find yourself wrestling with the following thoughts, renew your mind by meditating on the freedom facts and related truths from Scripture.

Baggage belief: I am alone and no one really cares how I feel or what I do.

Freedom fact: God is always with me. He sees how I feel, and He comforts me.

Truth of Scripture: "Cast all your anxiety on him because he cares for you" (1 Pet. 5:7, NIV). "The LORD himself goes before you and will be with you; he will never leave you nor forsake you. Do not be afraid; do not be discouraged" (Deut. 31:8, NIV).

Baggage belief: I'm not worth much. I don't deserve anything good.

Freedom fact: I have been blessed with every spiritual blessing. Because I am a child of God, I have an eternal inheritance in heaven.

Truth of Scripture: "Now we live with great expectation, and we have a priceless inheritance—an inheritance that is kept in heaven for you, pure and undefiled, beyond the reach of change and decay" (1 Pet. 1:3–4, NLT). "All praise to God, the Father of our Lord Jesus Christ, who has blessed us with every spiritual blessing in the heavenly realms because we are united with Christ" (Eph. 1:3, NLT).

Baggage belief: Because I have lived a lie, I am unable to speak truth.

Freedom fact: I can speak truth because I am led by the Spirit of God. There is freedom in living an honest life.

Truth of Scripture: "When he, the Spirit of truth, comes, he will guide you into all the truth. He will not speak on his own; he will speak only what he hears, and he will tell you what is yet to come" (John 16:13, NIV). "Then you will know the truth, and the truth will set you free" (John 8:32, NIV).

Baggage belief: God is going to have a hard time forgiving me for the things I have done and wrong choices I have made that hurt people.

Freedom fact: God delights to show grace. His forgiveness is endless, and His mercies are new every morning.

Truth of Scripture: "Who is a God like you, who pardons sin and forgives the transgression of the remnant of his inheritance?

You do not stay angry forever but delight to show mercy" (Mic. 7:18, NIV). "If we confess our sins, he is faithful and just and will forgive us our sins and purify us from all unrighteousness" (1 John 1:9, NIV).

∝§∾

Baggage belief: Not even God could love me after what I have been through.

Freedom fact: God loves me always, and nothing can separate me from His unfailing love. I choose to repent and turn to God.

Truth of Scripture: "I have loved you with an everlasting love; I have drawn you with unfailing kindness" (Jer. 31:3, NIV). "For I am convinced that neither death nor life, neither angels nor demons, neither the present nor the future, nor any powers, neither height nor depth, nor anything else in all creation, will be able to separate us from the love of God that is in Christ Jesus our Lord" (Rom. 8:38–39, NIV).

∝§∾

Baggage belief: I will never amount to anything because I was used and abused.

Freedom fact: I am more than a conqueror through Christ and have overcome the shame of my past. God has an amazing plan and purpose for my life, and He will give me the strength I need as I press toward it.

Truth of Scripture: "Forgetting what is behind and straining toward what is ahead, I press on toward the goal to win the prize for which God has called me heavenward in Christ Jesus" (Phil. 3:13–14, NIV). "But you belong to God, my dear children. You have already won a victory over those people, because the Spirit who lives in you is greater than the spirit who lives in the world"

(1 John 4:4, NLT). "'For I know the plans I have for you,' declares the LORD, 'plans to prosper you and not to harm you, plans to give you hope and a future'" (Jer. 29:11, NIV).

⚮

Baggage belief: I am doomed to live in fear that someone will take advantage of me again.

Freedom fact: God is my protector and is with me wherever I go. I will be confident because God will take care of me.

Truth of Scripture: "For God has not given us a spirit of fear and timidity, but of power, love, and self-discipline" (2 Tim. 1:7, NLT). "For the LORD your God is living among you. He is a mighty savior. He will take delight in you with gladness. With his love, he will calm all your fears" (Zeph. 3:17, NLT). "For our present troubles are small and won't last very long. Yet they produce for us a glory that vastly outweighs them and will last forever!" (2 Cor. 4:17, NLT).

⚮

Baggage belief: God's purpose and plan for my life has gone off track because I was hurt so badly.

Freedom fact: I am a child of God and nothing can change that! He has great plans for my life and is faithful to continue the good work He started in me.

Truth of Scripture: "Consider it pure joy, my brothers, whenever you face trials of many kinds, because you know that the testing of your faith produces perseverance. Let perseverance finish its work so that you may be mature and complete, not lacking anything" (James 1:2–4, NIV). "'For I know the plans I have for you,' says the LORD. 'They are plans for good and not for disaster, to give you a future and a hope'" (Jer. 29:11, NLT). "And

I am certain that God, who began the good work within you, will continue his work until it is finally finished on the day when Christ Jesus returns" (Phil. 1:6, NLT).

∾

Baggage belief: These emotions are so overwhelming I can't imagine ever getting over them.

Freedom fact: God cares how I feel, and He has great compassion toward me. I can rest in knowing that He will carry my burdens.

Truth of Scripture: "Give all your worries and cares to God, for he cares about you" (1 Pet. 5:7, NLT). "Yet the Lord longs to be gracious to you; therefore he will rise up to show you compassion. For the LORD is a God of justice" (Isa. 30:18, NIV). "For the LORD comforts his people and will have compassion on his afflicted ones" (Isa. 49:13, NIV).

∾

Baggage belief: I have been hurt so badly that I can never trust anyone again.

Freedom fact: God loves me, and I will trust Him no matter what. God will bring safe people into my life to love and encourage me in healthy ways.

Truth of Scripture: "Trust in the LORD with all your heart; do not depend on your own understanding" (Prov. 3:5, NLT). "To love him with all your heart, with all your understanding and with all your strength, and to love your neighbor as yourself is more important than all burnt offerings and sacrifices" (Mark 12:33, NIV). "If either of them falls down, one can help the other up. But pity anyone who falls and has no one to help them up" (Eccles. 4:10, NIV).

Baggage belief: No one will ever want me. I am "damaged goods."

Freedom fact: God has taken my shame and restored me to wholeness. I have confessed my sin to Him, and He has forgiven me and cleansed me. I am a virgin in God's eyes. I have been set free to enjoy my future!

Truth of Scripture: "He has sent me to bind up the broken-hearted, to proclaim freedom for the captives and release from darkness for the prisoners, to proclaim the year of the LORD's favor and the day of vengeance of our God, to comfort all who mourn, and provide for those who grieve in Zion—to bestow on them a crown of beauty instead of ashes, the oil of joy instead of mourning, and a garment of praise instead of a spirit of despair. They will be called oaks of righteousness, a planting of the LORD for the display of his splendor" (Isa. 61:1–3, NIV). "I have loved you with an everlasting love; I have drawn you with unfailing kindness. I will build you up again, and you, Virgin Israel, will be rebuilt. Again you will take up your timbrels and go out to dance with the joyful" (Jer. 31:3–4, NIV). "Arise, my darling, my beautiful one, come with me. See! The winter is past; the rains are over and gone" (Song of Sol. 2:10–11, NIV).

Baggage belief: No one—not even God—could ever love me after what I have been through.

Freedom fact: God loves me unconditionally, and nothing can separate me from His unfailing love.

Truth of Scripture: "I have loved you with an everlasting love; I have drawn you with unfailing kindness" (Jer. 31:3, NIV).

"For I am convinced that neither death nor life, neither angels nor demons, neither the present nor the future, nor any powers, neither height nor depth, nor anything else in all creation, will be able to separate us from the love of God that is in Christ Jesus our Lord" (Rom. 8:38–39, NIV). "Israel, put your hope in the LORD, for with the LORD is unfailing love and with him is full redemption" (Ps. 130:7, NIV).

Baggage belief: I must hold myself together and not share how I feel.

Freedom fact: God wants me to be real about how I feel so He can provide comfort and healing. It is when I am healed and whole that I can comfort others who have been through the same things I have.

Truth of Scripture: "Blessed are those who mourn, for they will be comforted" (Matt. 5:4, NIV). "Praise be to the God and Father of our Lord Jesus Christ, the Father of compassion and the God of all comfort, who comforts us in all our troubles, so that we can comfort those in any trouble with the comfort we ourselves receive from God" (2 Cor. 1:3–4, NIV).

Baggage belief: Since I was hurt by someone who was supposed to take care of me, no authority can be trusted.

Freedom fact: I will choose to obey those in authority over me because I know God places people in authority for my protection and not to hurt or control me. I trust that God will protect me as I submit with a willing heart, and I know that those who misuse their authority will answer to Him.

Truth of Scripture: "Let everyone be subject to the governing authorities, for there is no authority except that which God has established. The authorities that exist have been established by God" (Rom. 13:1, NIV). "Whatever you do, work at it with all your heart, as working for the Lord, not for human masters, since you know that you will receive an inheritance from the Lord as a reward. It is the Lord Christ you are serving. Anyone who does wrong will be repaid for their wrongs, and there is no favoritism" (Col. 3:23–25, NIV). "Obey your earthly masters with respect and fear, and with sincerity of heart, just as you would obey Christ. Obey them not only to win their favor when their eye is on you, but as slaves of Christ, doing the will of God from your heart" (Eph. 6:5–6, NIV).

Baggage belief: Sex is perverted and should never be enjoyed.

Freedom fact: Sex was God's idea. God created a man and a woman to enjoy sex within the boundaries of marriage. It is a beautiful expression of love that I will one day experience with my husband.

Truth of Scripture: "So God created mankind in his own image, in the image of God he created them; male and female he created them. God blessed them and said to them, 'Be fruitful and increase in number; fill the earth and subdue it'" (Gen. 1:27–28, NIV). The entire Book of Song of Songs (Solomon).

Baggage belief: If I act like nothing ever happened, the memories and emotions will eventually go away.

Freedom fact: I will speak out what is right, and I know God will be my refuge. I receive healing so that I no longer live in fear but can experience true peace.

Truth of Scripture: "I will heal my people and will let them enjoy abundant peace and security" (Jer. 33:6, NIV). "Have nothing to do with the fruitless deeds of darkness, but rather expose them" (Eph. 5:11, NIV). "My inmost being will rejoice when your lips speak what is right" (Prov. 23:16, NIV). "The one whose walk is blameless is kept safe, but the one whose ways are perverse will fall into the pit" (Prov. 28:18, NIV).

Baggage belief: If you knew the real me, you would reject me.

Freedom fact: With God's help, I can learn to be myself and trust Him to bring people into my life who will appreciate me and respect me for who I am. My worth is in who God says I am.

Truth of Scripture: "What's the price of two or three pet canaries? Some loose change, right? But God never overlooks a single one. And he pays even greater attention to you, down to the last detail—even numbering the hairs on your head! So don't be intimidated by all this bully talk. You're worth more than a million canaries" (Luke 12:6–7, THE MESSAGE). "God rescued us from dead-end alleys and dark dungeons. He's set us up in the kingdom of the Son he loves so much, the Son who got us out of the pit we were in, got rid of the sins we were doomed to keep repeating" (Col. 1:13–14, THE MESSAGE).

Baggage belief: Even when I do my best, it's not good enough. I can never meet the standard.

Freedom fact: I am fully loved, completely accepted, and totally pleasing to God. Regardless of how much I do or fail to do, I will remain fully loved, completely accepted, and totally pleasing to God. I choose to surrender to Him, trusting my faith in Him and His ability to sustain me. I will seek to be a God pleaser, not a people pleaser.

Truth of Scripture: "For I can do everything through Christ, who gives me strength" (Phil. 4:13, NLT). "Seek the Kingdom of God above all else, and live righteously, and he will give you everything you need" (Matt. 6:33, NLT).

Baggage belief: My life has always been full of turmoil. Some of my best years have already been wasted.

Freedom fact: God will restore all the time I have wasted or lost by my choices or the choices of others. God gives me peace.

Truth of Scripture: "I will restore to you the years that the swarming locust has eaten, the crawling locust, the consuming locust, and the chewing locust" (Joel 2:25, NKJV). "Peace I leave with you, My peace I give to you; not as the world gives do I give to you. Let not your heart be troubled, neither let it be afraid" (John 14:27, NKJV).

ABOUT THE AUTHOR

N ANCY ALCORN SPENT the first eight years of her career working for the state of Tennessee. Her time with the government included five years with the Department of Corrections working with juvenile delinquent girls, and three years with the Department of Human Services working in Emergency Protective Services investigating child abuse cases and supervising foster care.

It was during this time of government work that Nancy realized the inadequacy of these programs to offer real transformation in the lives of troubled individuals. Out of this experience came a driving passion for broken young girls that led to the birth of Mercy in 1983. Since that time, numerous residential and outreach programs have been established in various locations across America and other nations around the world. The ministry continues to grow and expand.

Nancy frequently speaks at conferences around the world, and in 2012 she was appointed to the Evangelical Council for Financial Accountability's Board of Reference, where she joined other prominent members such as Franklin Graham as an ambassador for financial accountability in leading Christian nonprofit organizations. She resides in Nashville, which is also the home of the international headquarters of Mercy.

NEED HELP?

Call confidentially today.

615.831.6987

At Mercy, no situation is hopeless!

If you are a young woman who is hopeless, desperate
and hurting—freedom and restoration are possible! Mercy is a
free-of-charge, Christian residential program that provides hope
and life transformation for young women ages 13-28 dealing with tough
issues such as abuse, eating disorders, self-harm, addiction, unplanned
pregnancy, and more. *There is no problem too big for God!*

If you or someone you know needs help, visit
MercyIntake.com or call **615.831.6987**.

Helpful Resources

Available Online at MercyMultiplied.com/Store

Issue-based books in our popular "Mercy For" Series include real-life stories of Mercy graduates, as well as practical advice and spiritual insight about life-controlling issues facing young women today. *Echoes of Mercy* and *Mission of Mercy* include Nancy Alcorn's personal journey to start Mercy. *Mercy Moves Mountains* contains stories of girls who have overcome!

We offer CDs and DVDs featuring Nancy Alcorn's powerful teachings on leadership, stewardship, forgiveness, walking in freedom and much more!

Every week, we tackle difficult, real-life issues with straight talk based on biblical wisdom and more than 30 years of experience. Topics range from sexual abuse and emotional healing to overcoming life-controlling issues and more!

These teachings are available on **iTunes** *and* **MercyTalk.org**.

For more information on Mercy and its global affiliates please visit **MercyMultiplied.com**.

For constant updates, follow us on social media!

FIND US ON FACEBOOK:
facebook.com/MercyMultiplied
facebook.com/NancyAlcorn

FIND US ON TWITTER:
twitter.com/MercyMultiplied
twitter.com/NancyAlcorn

FIND US ON BLOGSPOT:
NancyAlcorn.com

LISTEN TO OUR PODCAST:
MercyMultiplied.com/Media

Get Involved with
Mercy

You can play a key role in Mercy's ongoing work to restore the lives of young women in need! There are many ways to help. Join us today!

Attend.

Benefits, Luncheons, 5K Races, Nancy Alcorn's Speaking Engagements

Give.

Mercy 360, Sponsor A Girl, Planned Giving, Non-Cash Donations

Pray.

Join us in praying for Mercy staff, residents and graduates

Volunteer.

At Mercy Events, Homes or Corporate Headquarters; Internships

For more information, please visit
MercyMultiplied.com

Mercy...

First It's Something You Experience,
Then It's Something You Become.

Life is on-the-job training and sometimes the world can be a very cold and lonely place. You get by the best you can. You learn to make decisions as you go and you pay the price for bad ones. People judge you and label you—loser, dummy, junkie, or worse. Hope fades, darkness comes over you, and your dreams turn into nightmares.

But there's this thing called 'Mercy' that reaches in and shines a glimmer of light on that little piece of you that's still alive. It touches you and opens your eyes to a world of possibility. It's hard to explain. It's something you just have to experience. Mercy is a kind of forgiveness, of not being judged—but being accepted for who you *truly are* and who you *ultimately could be*—not the label you wear right now. It's love and kindness and caring on a level you never imagined!

Everyone had given up on me and I almost gave up on myself, but then I experienced Mercy and for the first time I felt that I mattered; that God had a plan for me and that somehow everything would be OK. I found myself in Mercy. It gave me hope and turned me around. I began to see myself and others differently. It changed me, and it keeps changing me every day. I'm learning the truth about life and I'm growing into the person I was meant to be. I'm not alone any more. I'm part of the Mercy Movement, the community of people whose hope has been restored and whose lives have been transformed; who don't stumble in the dark, but walk in the light. People who understand 'the Me in Mercy'.

So now I'm on a mission to live with a deeper meaning and purpose, to tell others the story of Mercy and me and to multiply its life-changing power in the world. Because the thing about Mercy is that first, it's something you experience, then it's something you become.

Mercy Multiplied
P.O. Box 111060
Nashville, TN 37222-1060

Phone: 615.831.6987 | Fax: 615.760.1113 | MercyMultiplied.com